The Rise of the Last Beast Kingdom

-

the Reason for Capitalism

The Rise of the Last Beast Kingdom

-

the Reason for Capitalism

by

One who loves GOD

ISBN: 9798848223217

Imprint: Independently published

SECOND EDITION

God is real

He created us and ALL

things

His name is YeHoVaH[1]*

---

¹ Genesis 6:2-3

 *God tells us His name in His Holy Scriptures. He NEVER tells us to call Him LORD, ADONAI, HaShem or any of the other manmade name used in the Bible. See Keith Johnson https://bfainternational.com for further understanding and information

We shall call Him by His name.

All biblical quotes herein are from the "Hebrew-English Tanakh The Jewish Bible", "The Complete Jewish Bible", "The NIV" or a combination thereof, with the true name of YeHoVaH inserted where appropriate.

Table of Contents

Foreword

This is written with the hope that all who read this book will come to know and worship our Creator – YeHoVaH. It is not a quick read and may take some time and effort, but it is worth it. YeHoVaH's love for us is beyond anything we know or have experienced. YeHoVaH created all things. He is the ONE and ONLY true GOD. He is God of Israel, which He created to be a light to the world and as a means of reintroducing Himself and His love to and for ALL people. He is the Father of Yeshua (Jesus) who is our salvation, our way/means of coming to our Father. This is a hope that you may read His Holy Scriptures – Torah, Prophets, Writings and the Gospel Record – praying that His Holy Spirit will guide you to His truth.

> 2 Corinthians 10: 3-5 "For although we do live in the world, we do not wage war in a worldly way; because the weapons we use to wage war are not worldly. On the contrary, they have God's power for demolishing strongholds. We demolish arguments and every arrogance that raises itself

up against the knowledge of God; we take every thought captive and make it obey the Messiah."

Pray and ask for His Holy Spirit to guide you in your walk and in your study.

May those who hold other beliefs, Judaism as taught by most Rabbis, Muslims, Hindus, Buddhist, those who practice man made Christianity (Catholicism /Protestants) and other religious or non religious beliefs, ***please know*** that as Yeshua tells us, He - Yeshua - is the only way to the Father and only those who do as our Father wishes will enter the coming kingdom (Mt 7:21-23). Many, probably most, of humanity rejects this and as human beings have done since our creation will replace the truth with a lie and hold to their basic belief that just being a "good" person is all they need to strive for. This is not the case. We have been told what we must do many times but we have refused each time. Time is up. YeHoVaH's time is here. YeHoVaH's time is now.

There is only ONE GOD – the Creator of ALL things. He is our Creator YeHoVaH - God of Israel, Father of Yeshua (Jesus). We know He is GOD as ***only He*** has told us the end at the beginning. He has done this that we may know and trust Him. By reading with His Holy Spirit guiding, may you be blessed and understand. YeHoVaH is Spirit but has been introduced to us in the masculine, so we address Him in the masculine and will do so herein.

We are currently living in the last world kingdom before the return of this world to our Creator – YeHoVaH, the ONE and ONLY GOD (Dt 4:32-36).   YeHoVaH is the Creator of ALL things known and unknown by human beings. He is the God of Israel and the Father of Yeshua. Yeshua is the only Messiah and has been given to ALL mankind for its salvation. By trusting and believing that Yeshua is the Son of YeHoVaH and that Yeshua is Messiah and Lord, we are blessed with salvation and enabled to enter into YeHoVaH's kingdom with everlasting life. The Scriptures' of YeHoVaH – the Torah, the Prophets, the Writings and the Gospel Record – show us the path which we need to follow. We are told of these things by YeHoVaH through His Holy Scriptures.

We are coming to the end of this world kingdom run by a system which has fooled the world. This is the last beast kingdom. The one which will dominate, devour, crush and condemn our souls. The one of which people will cry out, "Who can oppose the beast?" This last beast has been made so powerful through the introduction of capitalism. Capitalism has allowed all people to be fooled into thinking that money and creature comforts are the things that make this life worth living. This is the furthest thing from the truth. We are given life to enable us to know YeHoVaH and to come into His kingdom. We were not given life to be the slave of a system created to control us and empower and enrich an elite class who do not want to know God. This worldly existence is YeHoVaH's creation and He will not relinquish it. He has created a WAY for those that wish to join His Kingdom, simply - obey Torah, His Commands and trust that Yeshua is His Son/Messiah and Lord. All others who do not follow YeHoVaH's simple WAY are simply part of the manmade kingdom and its system that will be destroyed.

We are told of this end. It is time to understand and come to know His truth and the way we are to live and to teach our children to live during the short time remaining. No child born today (the year 2022) will live 50 years before the complete destruction of the current world kingdom and its system. The current world, or as we told in the Bible, beast system, is the culmination of the previous beast systems which have dominated our world and is the last.   This last beast kingdom was established and gained its strength through the imposition of what is known as capitalism.

There have been three primary previous world kingdoms, each with a system of control imposed by the elites. Each has been implemented by man and have all failed to follow the WORD we were given as to how we are to live together on this earth. Each has taken us further away from our Father. The current system is the most powerful and destructive to human kind. It has fooled the world by enslaving it in a system which creates a delusion that all needs can be met with monetary solutions that are presented as available to everyone. Rather than seeking justice and righteousness, it makes these afterthoughts to making money to "support oneself and family". It makes ones goal to seek earthly riches rather than trusting and relying on God as we are suppose to as told to us in His WORD. This beast system has the world dealing with the loss of human life so cavalierly that holding sports events and opening the economy are more important than saving the lives (souls) of other people, our brothers and sisters. It has people so confused they do not love each other as we are called to do; rather they have divided themselves in manmade groups based on color, class, gender, all things that have NO importance at all. The governing bodies of the greatest economic and political powers in the world are concerned about and deal with any tragedy simply because it results in less money being produced. We can only be glad that it will be ending soon. Tragically, many will see the ending of this beast system with its capitalism as a bad thing, not understanding that it enables the system which prevents us from living life as our Father intended.

GOD exists. We observe this everyday in seeing all He has created. He has created ALL THINGS and identified Himself through His Holy Scriptures - Torah, the Writings, the Prophets and the Gospel Record. He is YeHoVaH - identified God of Israel, Father of His Son - Yeshua (Jesus) the ONLY Messiah. YeHoVaH created ALL things, the heavens with all matter therein above and the earth and seas below. There should be NO doubt or question about this. All thinking, reasoning beings can come to this conclusion upon approaching it with an open mind. There is no scientific evidence which supports any other conclusion. Those that claim there is distort, contort and resort to changes of the actual true world findings that YeHoVaH has enabled us to discover, as He tells us He will, in order that we may believe and trust in Him. Unfortunately from the very beginning the beings He created to steward His creation-we human beings- failed to obey that which He told us to do. This failure to obey led to the establishment of the man created kingdoms run by systems developed to dominate and subjugate all others by an elite which holds itself to be in place of God. This course of events is told to us by YeHoVaH in His Scriptures.

Many today do not believe in the truth of His Holy Scriptures. The same spirit which caused mankind to disobey YeHoVaH in the Garden of Eden continued, resulting in the Flood, resulting in the Confusion of Language and continues today. As in the time after the Flood and before the Confusion of Language, mankind today seeks to formulate their own answers from the world around them rather than trusting in our Creator. People look in the wrong place for the truth they are seeking to find. Unfortunately the methods used today in science, anthropology, physics etc. are not questioned. People assume the information that is given has been substantiated by an undisputable method. If those who provide the information are completely honest, they will admit there are assumptions they make in arriving at the conclusions they set forth. They use circular arguments. NONE of these assumptions can be demonstrated to be "true" without the use of another assumption which by itself is also unproven.

We are currently living in the last of the manmade kingdoms run by a system controlled by an elite through money produced by capitalism. As we have been told, this system is going to be destroyed along with most of the people living on this planet. One's only hope is to repent and trust and obey YeHoVaH. This means obeying His Commands, accepting His Son Yeshua (Jesus) as the ONLY Messiah and Lord and loving YeHoVaH and each other. We show our love of YeHoVaH by loving each other and obeying His Holy WORD. This means more than giving to charity and considering yourself a "good person". We must walk the narrow pass told to us by Yeshua. Obey Torah and the Commands of YeHoVaH.

This work is produced in hope that all that may will follow as we have been told. It seeks to lay out our history in broad strokes using the Holy Scriptures as the true guide post. The WORD of YeHoVaH is true.

This is a book of HOPE and INSPIRATION not fear.

Let us examine what has occurred and look to come to the understanding that will help us to surrender to our Father and be part of the kingdom He will usher in.

May we all know the love and salvation of Yeshua – HalleluYah!!!

Chapter I

GOD's WORD is TRUE

Psalm 119:160 *"The main thing about Your word is that it's true; and all Your just rulings last forever."*

As we are told here and elsewhere in the Psalms and other WORDS of His Scripture, YeHoVaH's WORD is true. One of the ways He demonstrates to us that His WORD is true and that He is real is by telling us the future before it happens. YeHoVaH is the ONLY GOD that proclaims this ability and the ONLY One to demonstrate it. In reiterating this fact He tells us:

Isaiah 46:9-10 "Remember things that happened at the beginning, long ago — that I am God, and there is no other; I am God, and there is none like me. At the beginning I announce the end, proclaim in advance things not yet done; and I say that my plan will hold, I will do everything I please to do."

One of the most dramatic and incontrovertible events He tells us of, is the rebuilding of the Temple built by Solomon and the reestablishment of Israel and the city of Jerusalem.

After the establishment of the state of Israel, YeHoVaH told His chosen ruler David that David's son would build YeHoVaH's Temple (2 Samuel 7). As YeHoVaH had declared, David's son Solomon went on to build this Temple. It was in the 480th year after the people of Israel had left the land of Egypt (966 BCE), in the fourth year of Solomon's reign over Israel, in the second month, that Solomon began to build the house of YeHoVaH (1 Kings 6:1, 1 Kings 6:38).

This Temple and Israel with Jerusalem itself would later be destroyed by King Nebuchadnezzar in 605 BCE. In

538 BCE, Cyrus the Great ended the Israel exile, allowing the Temple to be restored and Jerusalem to be rebuilt. These are verifiable historical events.[2]

God foretold these very things. These events were told of primarily through His Prophet Isaiah. Isaiah's prophecies were between the years 739 BCE to 701 BCE.[3] These prophecies were pronounced *96 years prior to the destruction of the Temple built by Solomon along with the capture and destruction of Israel and the city of Jerusalem.* YeHoVaH through His WORD, told us that this destruction would occur. He also foretold who would authorize the Temple to be rebuilt and the reestablishment of Jerusalem as a city. YeHoVaH told all that this person would be Cyrus the Great, *106 years prior to Cyrus' birth.*

> **Isaiah 44:23-28** "Sing, you heavens, for YeHoVaH has done it! Shout, you depths of the earth! Mountains, break out into song, along with

---

[2] Britannica, The Editors of Encyclopaedia. "Temple of Jerusalem summary". *Encyclopedia Britannica*, 14 Oct. 2003, https://www.britannica.com/summary/Temple-of-Jerusalem. Accessed 19 August 2022.
[3] Isaiah Bible Timeline (biblehub.com)

every tree in the forest! For YeHoVaH has redeemed Jacob; He glorifies Himself in Israel. Here is what YeHoVaH says, your Redeemer, He who formed you in the womb: "I am YeHoVaH, who makes all things, who stretched out the heavens all alone, who spread out the earth all by myself. I frustrate false prophets and their omens, I make fools of diviners, I drive back the sages and make their wisdom look silly. I confirm My servants' prophecies and make My messengers' plans succeed. I say of Jerusalem: 'She will be lived in,' of the cities of Judah, 'They will be rebuilt; I will restore their ruins.' I say to the deep sea, 'Dry up! I will make your streams run dry.' I say of Cyrus, 'He is My shepherd, he will do everything I want. He will say of Jerusalem, "You will be rebuilt," and of the temple, "Your foundation will be laid."'"

Continuing

Isaiah 45:1-7 "Thus says YeHoVaH to Cyrus, His anointed, whose right hand He has grasped, so that He subdues nations before him and strips kings of their robes, so that doors open in front of him, and no gates are barred:"I will go ahead of you, leveling the hills, shattering the bronze gates, smashing the iron bars. I will give you treasures hoarded in the dark, secret riches hidden away, so that you will know that I, YeHoVaH, calling you by your name, am the God of Israel. It is for the sake of Jacob My servant, yes, for

Israel My elect, that I call you by your name and give you a title, although you don't know Me. I am YeHoVaH; there is no other; besides Me there is no God. I am arming you, although you don't know Me, so that those from the east and those from the west will know that there is none besides Me — I am YeHoVaH; there is no other. I form light, I create darkness; I make well-being, I create woe; I, YeHoVaH, do all these things."

YeHoVaH's WORD is true. Cyrus went forth as YeHoVaH said he would and Jerusalem and the Temple built by Solomon were rebuilt upon Cyrus' instruction. YeHoVaH foretold things in the past which did occur just as He said they would. He has foretold things in our future that will also occur as He says they will. Come to know His truth and love.

Let us now go forth and TRUST His WORD.

Chapter II

Governing System

YeHoVaH loves us and His Word is truth. His love provides all things needed for our existence with Him. The act of creation itself was the demonstration of this love. He made us in His image and thus included within us a natural ability to love and a desire for freedom. Our failure and/or inability to return His love by simply obeying the one Command He originally gave us resulted in the governing systems which developed in the past and continue to this current and last manmade system under which we now live. This system,   continuing in the way it began, is an attempt to take the One True God out of our conscience, out of existence and replace Him with a manmade slavery system intended to glorify and benefit those few at the top who wish to be gods themselves. They ignore YeHoVaH's truth and claim there is no God. The society and system they have made are constantly attempting to indoctrinate us and replace YeHoVaH's truth with lies about evolution or any other thought, method or philosophy used to explain our world. The idea that man is naturally a "good being" and as such does not need God or at best only needs to follow God's moral code is continually pushed. For those who will not go that far, the ruling elites push the "all gods are the same" lie. If this lie does not fit, they push the "genius of men will provide the way" view. In actuality, there is only ONE God and our failure to recognize and obey Him has resulted in the world as we know it today. God is Spirit and is presented to us in His WORD in the masculine and thus is presented that way. His love for us is so great that He has provided a way for us to return to Him. YeHoVaH promises:

> ***2 Chronicles 7:13-14***[4] *"If I shut up heaven that there be no rain, or if I command the locust to devour the land, or if I send pestilence among My people, if My people, who call on My name, shall humble themselves,* and *pray, and seek My face, and turn from their evil ways; then will I hear from heaven, and will forgive their sin, and will heal their land."*

---

[4] All biblical quotes are from the "Hebrew-English Tanakh The Jewish Bible", "The Complete Jewish Bible", "The NIV" or a combination of thereof with the true name of YeHoVaH inserted where appropriate.

AND

> *Luke 24: 44-47* " *Yeshua said to them, "This is what I meant when I was still with you and told you that everything written about me in the Torah of Moshe, the Prophets and the Psalms had to be fulfilled." Then he opened their minds, so that they could understand the Tanakh, telling them, "Here is what it says: the Messiah is to suffer and to rise from the dead on the third day; and in his name repentance leading to forgiveness of sins is to be proclaimed to people from all nations, starting with Jerusalem."*

Trust that as Yeshua tells us in Matthew 7:21 those who do as our Father wants will enter into His Kingdom.

After our creation had we obeyed YeHoVaH's Commands, God's natural governing system would have been put in place among humankind. As we are told, love YeHoVaH and love our neighbor. With each person loving YeHoVaH and loving their neighbor as themselves, equality amongst all people would have developed. This system would have been a self governing system with our Creator at the head and each person living in love with his neighbor. This is what we can look forward to.

Upon our creation we were given all things needed to live and flourish with God.

> ***Genesis 1:26-28*** *"Then God said, "Let us make mankind in our image, in the likeness of ourselves; and let them rule over the fish in the sea, the birds in the air, the animals, and over all the earth, and over every crawling creature that crawls on the earth." So God created mankind in His own image; in the image of God He created him: male and female He created them. God blessed them: God said to them, "Be fruitful, multiply, fill the earth and subdue it. Rule over the fish in the sea, the birds in the air and every living creature that crawls on the earth."*

Continuing

__Genesis 1: 29-31__"And God said: 'Behold, I have given you every herb yielding seed, which is upon the face of all the earth, and every tree, in which is the fruit of a tree yielding seed—to you it shall be for food; and to every beast of the earth, and to every fowl of the air, and to everything that creepeth upon the earth, wherein there is a living soul, every green herb for food.' And it was so. And God saw everything that He had made, and, behold, it was very good. And there was evening and there was morning, the sixth day"

YeHoVaH made all things needed by man and woman to live and thrive with Him on earth. With His love we had all things. God's love given to us is to be returned to Him and shared by us with each other. God gave Adam, the first human being, one Command - No one was to eat from the tree of the knowledge of good and evil.

__Genesis 2:15-17__"And YeHoVaH God took the man and put him into the Garden of Eden to dress it and to keep it. And YeHoVaH God commanded the man, saying: 'Of every tree of the garden thou may freely eat but of the tree of the knowledge of good and evil, *thou shall not eat of it; for in the day that thou eatest thereof thou shall surely die.'"*

We had received God's commandment.

YeHoVaH provided all which was needed and gave us the ability to choose. We had the choice to obey or not. We chose not to obey. We did not obey.

> **Genesis 3:6** *"And when the woman saw that the tree was good for food, and that it was a delight to the eyes, and that the tree was to be desired to make one wise, she took of the fruit thereof, and did eat; and she gave also unto her husband with her, and he did eat."*

Having failed to obey our Creator, we forfeited the opportunity to live in love and harmony with our God on this earth at that time.

> **Genesis 3:17-19** *"And unto Adam He said: 'Because thou hast hearkened unto the voice of thy wife, and hast eaten of the tree, of which I commanded thee,*

saying: Thou shalt not eat of it; cursed is the ground for thy sake; in toil shalt thou eat of it all the days of thy life. Thorns also and thistles shall it bring forth to thee; and thou shalt eat the herb of the field. In the sweat of thy face shalt thou eat bread, till thou return unto the ground; for out of it wast thou taken; for dust thou art, and unto dust shalt thou return.'"

The first time we did not obey the Command of our Father and we are told of the consequences we are to suffer.

Genesis 3:22-24 *"And YeHoVaH God said: 'Behold, the man is become as one of us, to know good and evil; and now, lest he put forth his hand, and take also of the tree of life, and eat, and live forever.' Therefore YeHoVaH God sent him forth from the Garden of Eden, to till the ground from whence he was taken. So He drove out the man; and He placed at the east of the Garden of Eden the cherubim, and the flaming sword which turned every way, to keep the way to the tree of life."*

Having failed to obey our Father, we lost the chance to live with YeHoVaH under the original governing system which YeHoVaH established. We lost the opportunity to live under His governing system in which we were to trust and live with each other in love. Instead, man would set up a governing system, establishing the way we live together. Ultimately mankind would develop governing systems which did not include trusting and obeying our Creator or loving Him above all else or each other. We as His creations instead instituted a system of dominance one over another. This system which requires and is based upon the will of one person dominating that of another is what we established and how we govern ourselves instead of trusting and following the Commandments of YeHoVaH.

With the failure of humankind to trust, acknowledge and obey our Creator, we set up the human governing systems. Failing to obey the Command of YeHoVaH we failed to love each other. After being taken out of the Garden, man began the pattern of interaction which continues to this day and resulted in the formation of the current beast system in which we live. The first human being born after our creation established the pattern which enabled our current system to develop and be put in place.

Chapter III

The First World Governing System

Cain was the first born of the two created human beings, Adam and his wife Eve. Adam and Eve then had a second son, Abel. The two boys lived together each going about their respective tasks. Cain became upset with Abel. Rather than loving his brother as himself, Cain became distraught. YeHoVaH saw this in Cain and told Cain that Cain did not have to feel this way and could control himself.

Genesis 4:6-8 *"YeHoVaH said to Cain, "Why are you angry? Why so downcast? If you are doing what is good, shouldn't you hold your head high? And if you don't do what is good, sin is crouching at the door— it wants you, **but you can rule over it**. (emphasis added)"Cain had words with Abel his brother; then one time, when they were in the field, Cain turned on Abel his brother and killed him."*

Cain did not heed the WORD of YeHoVaH. The first human being born after creation kills his brother. He did not obey YeHoVaH and Cain killed Abel. Even when warned and given the knowledge that he could resist doing his brother harm and not succumb to sin, *trust* and *obedience* to YeHoVaH's WORD was rejected. Rather than interact with his brother with love, Cain became the first to exert his will over another person's, his brother, to do that which he wanted done. Rather than obeying God, Cain made his own rule on how to interact with someone else. This established the manner in which humankind would craft its own laws for interactions between people to the present day.

The killing of Abel by his brother Cain, this rejection of YeHoVaH, established the pattern of and led to the establishment of the first system of government by men. One human being through force dominates another and establishes manmade rules of behavior as the manner of interaction between people. With the decision not to obey the Commands of God came the domination one person over another and the creation of manmade rules of behavior and ultimately the governing style and principals we live by. Continuing this pattern, within a few generations, the introduction of polygamy by Cain's ancestor was made and became practice. Again, a manmade behavior in place of the way told to us and set up by God. YeHoVaH created one woman to be bound with one man.

Genesis 2:18-25 *"YeHoVaH, God, said, "It isn't good that the person should be alone. I will make for him a companion suitable for helping him." So from the ground YeHoVaH, God, formed every wild animal and every bird that flies in the air, and he brought them to the person to see what he would call them. Whatever the person would call each living creature, that was to be its name. So the person gave names to all the livestock, to the birds in the air and to every wild animal. But for Adam there was not found a companion suitable for helping him. Then God caused a deep sleep to fall upon the person; and while he was sleeping, he took one of his ribs and closed up the place from which he took it with flesh. And with the rib which YeHoVaH, God, had taken from the person, he made a woman-person; and he brought her to the man-person. The man-person said, "At last! This is bone from my bones and flesh from my flesh. She is to be called*

Polygamy was, once again, men failing to trust and obey God and establishing a practice man chose. Polygamy and other manmade rules were established and followed as the earth's population proliferated. Cain's relatives killed other people. With this continual failure to trust and obey the WORD of YeHoVaH, sin and the spread of wickedness expanded throughout the land. This wide spreading of evil resulted in the Great Flood. This event consumed all humankind except Noah and his family, ending the society which began with the failure to obey YeHoVaH's first Command and His warning to Cain which resulted in that governing system that was used by Cain's descendants and the rest of humankind.

Genesis 6:5-8 *"YeHoVaH saw that the people on earth were very wicked, that all the imaginings of their hearts were always of evil only. YeHoVaH regretted that He had made mankind on the earth;*

it grieved His heart. YeHoVaH said, "I will wipe out humankind, whom I have created, from the whole earth; and not only human beings, but animals, creeping things and birds in the air; for I regret that I ever made them." But Noah found grace in the sight of YeHoVaH."

The failure of our forefather to obey our Creator not only took us out of the Garden, it took away the order by which we were to live together. YeHoVaH removed us from the Garden for this transgression to prevent any attempt to obtain the fruit of eternal life. Had we eaten of that fruit, we would have been permanently excluded from the kingdom of God as we would have been eternally evil with no hope of redemption. YeHoVaH prevented the further falling away from Him with the intent of enabling us by His love for us to be saved. Our Creator has always provided a way back to Him. At each stage when we have rejected His WORD, YeHoVaH has directly intervened in human events with a warning and message to turn back to Him with love and OBEDIENCE. For His love for us is great. As is set forth in 1Corinthians 2:9

1Corinthians 2:9 *"But, as the Tanakh says, "No eye has seen, no ear has heard and no one's heart has imagined all the things that God has prepared for those who love him.""*

We have always fallen short, however. Man's actions then develop into the human methods by which to live with one another and which then lead to the governing systems established.

Even though it pained YeHoVaH to move as He did, YeHoVaH's love for human kind resulted in the flood. Our Creator wishes that ALL who may, will join with Him. He has always provided and shown us the Way but few take the narrow path. His way is higher than our way and His knowledge greater than ours.

Isaiah 55:6 -11 *"Seek YeHoVaH while He is available, call on Him while He is still nearby. Let the wicked person abandon his way and the evil person his thoughts; let him return to YeHoVaH, and He will have mercy on him; let him return to our God, for He will freely forgive. "For My thoughts are*

*not your thoughts, and your ways are not My ways,"
says YeHoVaH. "As high as the sky is above the earth
are My ways higher than your ways, and My
thoughts than your thoughts. For just as rain and
snow fall from the sky and do not return there, but
water the earth, causing it to bud and produce,
giving seed to the sower and bread to the eater; so is
My word that goes out from My mouth—it will not
return to Me unfulfilled; but it will accomplish what
I intend, and cause to succeed what I sent it to do."*

YeHoVaH's love for us is great and available to all who
seek it and trust and obey His WORD.

Psalm 96:1-3" Sing to YeHoVaH a new song!
Sing to YeHoVaH, all the earth!
Sing to YeHoVaH, bless His name!
Proclaim His victory day after day!
Declare His glory among the nations,
His wonders among all peoples!"

HalleluYah!!!

Chapter IV

The Flood

The failure of man to trust and obey the Commands of YeHoVaH resulted in the first of mankind being corrupt and filled with violence. To end this corruption, YeHoVaH flooded the entire world.

Genesis 6:17-22 *""Then I myself will bring the flood of water over the earth to destroy from under heaven every living thing that breathes; everything on earth will be destroyed. But I will establish My covenant with you; you will come into the ark, you, your sons, your wife and your sons' wives with you. "From everything living, from each kind of living being, you are to bring two into the ark, to keep them alive with you; they are to be male and female. Of each kind of bird, each kind of livestock, and each kind of animal creeping on the ground, two are to come to you, so that they can be kept alive. Also take from all the kinds of food that are eaten, and collect it for yourself; it is to be food for you and for them." This is what Noah did; he did all that God ordered him to do."*

And after Noah obeyed YeHoVaH and built the Ark and the animals were on it, the Flood came.

Genesis 7:17-19 "And the flood was forty days upon the earth; and the waters increased, and bore up the ark, and it was lifted up above the earth. And the waters prevailed, and increased greatly upon the earth; and the ark went upon the face of the waters. And the waters prevailed exceedingly upon the earth; and all the high mountains that were under the whole heaven were covered."

After the flooding had stopped and the land dried, YeHoVaH directed Noah and his family to leave the Ark. Noah left and immediately gave thanks to our Father.

Genesis 8:20 "And Noah builded an altar unto the YeHoVaH; and took of every clean beast, and of every clean fowl, and offered burnt-offerings on the altar.

Noah immediately went out of the Ark after settling on the dry land and thanked YeHoVaH. He made a sacrificial offering to YeHoVaH, demonstrating and continuing the practice of worshipping our Creator. This was the first thing he did, give honor and glory to our GOD. All people living on earth today are descendants of the family of Noah.[5] This is why all the manmade religions of the world seem similar. Each group took the basics from that which Noah did and applied them to their particular group.

The truth of the Bible has been and continues to be confirmed by the archeological evidence that has been discovered in the past and continues to be found to this day. The Flood is one example of this fact. It is ironic that those who today seek to discredit the Bible, or propose it is just stories giving people a moral compass

---

[5] See New DNA Study Confirms Noah **BY** <u>**BRIAN THOMAS, PH.D. ***</u> **| MONDAY, MAY 16, 2016**

See also: www.astirinch.com/creation/dna-proof-of-noahs-flood/

with which to follow, have made and are making these discoveries. Unfortunately instead of these discoveries opening their eyes, most of them use misplaced assumptions and still use the findings to support their erroneous denial of the Bible. One such finding is the "Ice Age". The "Ice Age" occurred after the Flood. The findings of the emergence of what is collectively know by archeologists as "civilization" is said to have begun after the "Ice Age". The fact that there were vast areas of the earth covered by glaciers is not disputed. The cause of this phenomenon however cannot be explained by the secular community of scientists. By examining the evidence without prejudice, we see that the evidence at hand as presented, without supposition, is consistent with the Biblical record. The Flood resulted in the world being capable of developing the ice caps which appeared at that time after the Flood.[6]

---

[6] What caused Ice Age - creation.com; NOAH'S FLOOD EXPLAINS ICE AGE | LIVING ETERNAL NOW

Chapter V

Post Flood – The Beginning of Civilization

After the waters that created the Flood stopped, the waters resided and the Ark came to rest in the mountains of Arafat. Noah and his family then left the Ark and walked onto dry land. After Noah had given thanks and made an offering to YeHoVaH, YeHoVaH then established a covenant with Noah, his descendents and all living creatures on the Ark.

Genesis 9:8-17 "And God spoke unto Noah, and to his sons with him, saying: 'As for Me, behold, I establish My covenant with you, and with your seed after you; and with every living creature that is with you, the fowl, the cattle, and every beast of the earth with you; of all that go out of the ark, even every beast of the earth. And I will establish My covenant with you; neither shall all flesh be cut off any more by the waters of the flood; neither shall there anymore be a flood to destroy the earth.' And God said: 'This is the token of the covenant which I make between Me and you and every living creature that is with you, for perpetual generations: I have set My bow in the cloud, and it shall be for a token of a covenant between Me and the earth. And it shall come to pass, when I bring clouds over the earth, and the bow is seen in the cloud, that I will remember My covenant, which is between Me and you and every living creature of all flesh; and the waters shall no more become a flood to destroy all flesh. And the bow shall be in the cloud; and I will look upon it, that I may remember the everlasting covenant between God and every living creature of all flesh that is upon the earth.' And God said unto Noah: 'This is the token of the covenant which I have established between Me and all flesh that is upon the earth.'"

HalleluYah!!!

After Noah's offering of thanks and YeHoVaH's blessing, Noah, his wife, his sons Shem, Ham, Japheth and their wives began their life in the area of Arafat which encompasses the Gordyaen Mountains in southeast

Turkey.[7] The place of Noah and his family's original settlement is Thamanin.[8]

The archeological finds to this day that are used in declaring the beginning of "civilization" also support the accuracy and truthfulness of the Bible. The finds made by the archeologists, in the chronological order established by the finds, are completely consistent with the biblical record. The archeologists have dated their finds incorrectly however, as they use methods of dating which they need to support their narrative of a billion or some number year old earth. They make these statements on age but fail to state the fact that these numbers are derived by assumptions based on assumptions. They CANNOT prove any of the assumptions they make, yet they continue to spread the falsehoods of a million/billion plus year old earth. Without their dates, and taking the findings in chronological order, the undisputed findings themselves match the biblical record.[9]

---

[7] Ararat or Judi? | Search for Noah's Ark (arksearch.com)
[8] Shlama - The Shade of the Ark
[9] The Big Dating Blunder by Jonathan Gray Microsoft Word - DATING BOOK.doc (beforeus.com);The Lost Races – the Big Dating Shock by Jonathan Gray p. 25-27 Microsoft Word - DATING OF CIVILIZATIONS.doc (beforeus.com)

This begins with where the Ark came to rest. As stated in the Bible, the Ark came to rest in the mountains of Ararat (Genesis 8:4). Some consider the biblical expression *mountains of Ararat* to have its full plural meaning to include the *mountains of Urartu*.[10] It is believed that the land of "Ararat" is the Hebrew equivalent of Urardhu, or Urartu[11]. The remains of Noah's Ark have been discovered adjacent to the Kurdish village of Uzengili, Turkey.[12]   In this area a settlement was also discovered. The settlement has been identified as Thamanin. Thamanin is the place where Noah and his family established as their initial home.[13] It has been identified as the location of the oldest settlement in the world.[14] This area near the foot of Mount Judi (or Mount Cudi) is identified in some of the earliest sources as the place of the landing of the Ark and Thamanin as the settlement founded by the survivors of the Flood.[15] The declaration of Thamanin as the original settlement of Noah and his descendents is strengthened by more scientific arguments, connected with the etymology of place-names around Judi. Early Arabic sources mention a village called Thamanin, built by Noah at the foot of

---

[10] Shlama - The Shade of the Ark
[11] What is ARARAT? - WebBible Encyclopedia - ChristianAnswers.Net
[12] www.noahsarksearch.com/davedeal.htm
[13] Shlama - The Shade of the Ark
[14] Discovering the Lost City of Thamanin (sccompton.com)
[15] *Locating the City of Thamanin by S.C. Compton*

Mount Judi. This Semitic name can refer to the number 8, i.e. the eight persons who according to Genesis came out of the Ark: Noah, his wife and their three sons with their wives[16]

Noah and his family began life at Thamanin after the Flood. From here, the beginning of what is called "civilization" began to develop after the Flood. The archeological records demonstrate that the first settlements are all found in the area where Noah's Ark came to rest. The periods immediately after the Flood and prior to the Confusion of Languages have been classified by archeologists. Their erroneous dating causes many to think the occurrences' during these periods fall outside the biblical narrative. Ignoring the dates set forth by these archeologists, their findings are consistent with and actually confirm the Bible record. The period said to be the "stone age" includes the Paleolithic, Neolithic and a portion of the Chalcolithic periods. During these periods, there is the development of the Halaf, Hassuna and Samarra cultures. These were the periods when Noah's descendants established the area where they initially lived, Thamanin, and moved

---

[16] Shlama - The Shade of the Ark

from this area. The time historians and archeologists call the "beginning of civilization".

After Thamanin was settled, more and more of the descendants of Noah began to move north and south. The movement was into the Anatolia, the Caucasus, the area south and north near current day Lake Van and the area including the fertile valley of the Khabur River which became known as North or Northern Mesopotamia. Anatolia is located and encompasses the area surrounding current day Turkey, the area known as Asia Minor. The earliest representations of culture in Anatolia can be found in several archaeological sites located in the central and eastern part of the region. Stone Age artifacts such as animal bones and food fossils were found at Burdur (north of Antalya).[17] As the communities continued to grow the settlements entered into and through what the archeologist call the Paleolithic and Neolithic and Chalcolithic periods. One of the first what are called "hunter/gathers settlements attributed to these periods have been discovered in Anatolia.[18]

---

[17] *www.peraair.com/timeline-and-history-of-asia-minor-anatolia*
[18] "Anatolia and the Caucasus, 8000–2000 B.C." In Heilbrunn Timeline of Art History. New York: The Metropolitan Museum of Art, 2000–. http://www.metmuseum.org/toah/ht/?period=02®ion=waa (October

As the population continued to grow during these periods, settlements developed with cultural identities. The earliest settlements experienced the development of what has been identified by archeologists as the Halaf, Hassuna and Samarra cultures. These cultures have been found along the Euphrates and Tigress Rivers in the area identified as Mesopotamia and identified in the Bible as Shinar. The Halaf culture was named after the site of Tel Halaf, in the Khabur Valley in north-eastern Syria, where it was first identified. Located south of the Ark's resting place, its cultural findings are consistent with those of the Paleolithic, Neolithic and Chalcolithic periods.[19]

In a location just southeast of the Halaf was found what is referred to as the Hassuna culture. Both were very similar. They have been classified by current day archeologists as Neolithic archaeological cultures. These settlements are located in what is called by archeologists as Northern Mesopotamia. Halaf-influenced material is found throughout

2000)
[19] *Mario Liverani (2013). The Ancient Near East: History, Society and Economy. p. 48. ISBN 9781134750849.*

Greater Mesopotamia.[20]   The Samara culture overlaps
the Hassuna culture and included an area just south of
the Hassuna. The Samarra culture is a Late
Neolithic archaeological culture of northern
Mesopotamia. It partially overlaps with Hassuna and
early Ubaid.[21] These findings are completely consistent
with what we are told in the Bible as the descendents of
Noah moved from Thamanin south into Shinar identified
by archeologists as Mesopotamia.

The continued growth of the human population saw the
continual development of the Halaf, Hassuna and
Samarra cultures which led to the Ubaid culture's
development in these areas. The Ubaid period is the
designation used by archeologists for the period of
"prehistory of Mesopotamia". The Ubaid refers to a time
period and the material culture exhibited
in Mesopotamia and adjacent areas which predate the
rise of the great urban cities.[22] This occurred during
what is termed the Chalcolithic, a period where stone
tools were found along with the cooper and bronze tools
and artifacts.[23] While studying Tel al-Ubaid, the site of a

---

[20] https://en.wikipedia.org/wiki/Halaf_culture
[21] Samarra culture — Wikipedia Republished // WIKI 2
[22] Hirst, K. Kris. "Ubaidian Culture." ThoughtCo, Feb. 16, 2021,
thoughtco.com/ubaidian-culture-ubaid-roots-mesopotamia-173089.

Sumerian city, Assyriologist Charles Leonard Woolley concludes that the Sumerian culture came directly after a less developed culture, a culture that most likely made up the first people to settle and grow crops on the southern Mesopotamia plain.[24] The findings of the archeologists suggest that the people lived peacefully with each other, and initially during this period, there were no real findings of an elite within the settlements. This too is consistent with the biblical record as immediately after the Flood people were still in harmony living and worshipping YeHoVaH.

The group of Noah's family that stayed in the area around Thamanin began spreading throughout the immediate area eventually becoming the Ararat kingdom. Urartu was often called the "Kingdom of Ararat" in many ancient manuscripts and holy writings of different nations.[25] The Ubaid culture grew and included these descendants of Noah who stayed closer to Thamanin and established settlements in the area in and around current day Lake Van. As the families grew they spread within this area, people lived primarily in small hamlets or one or two largish towns. The Kingdom of

---

[23] http://www.worldhistory.biz/ancient-h...
[24] Ib-http://www.worldhistory.biz/ancient-h
[25] **Urartu** - armeniapedia.org

Urartu was established in this area, situated in a mountainous area near Lake Van.[26] This is thought to have occurred during what many call the "Ubaid period". The Ubaid material culture, including ceramic decorative styles, artifact types and architectural forms, existed over the vast Near Eastern region between the Mediterranean to the Straits of Hormuz, including parts of Anatolia and perhaps the Caucasus mountains.[27] As we are told in the Bible, over time, other groups moved from the initial settlement throughout the region spreading south into Shinar, what has become to be known as Mesopotamia. During this initial move, all people continue to speak one language and worship YeHoVaH. As years past, new generations continued to spread out across the area. This region spans in all directions north and south - east and west of the area where the Ark which carried Noah and his descendants rested.   The finding of Noah's Ark in this area, the various settlements found in this area and extending all the way to the Persian Gulf, up through the Caucus Mountains and beyond, and to the Aegean Sea again confirms the WORD of YeHoVaH. His Scripture tells us of the

[26] (Plotrovsky, 1969; pg 43. - Plotrovsky, B. 1969. **The ancient civilization of Urartu.** Cowles Book Co. New York. PP. 1-224. Translated from the Russian by James Hogarth.)
[27] Hirst, K. Kris. "Ubaidian Culture." ThoughtCo, Feb. 16, 2021, thoughtco.com/ubaidian-culture-ubaid-roots-mesopotamia-173089.)

establishment of the area by Noah and his family as well as the spreading out of people into these areas after the Flood.

Chapter VI

The Tower of Babel and the Confusion of Language

The development of the Halaf, Hassuana and Samarra cultures and the emergence of the Ubaid culture saw communities enlarge; this enlargement leading to the Uruk period.[28] At this point larger groups formed and moved south further into Shinar where the settlement of Uruk was established by Nimrod. This area took on characteristics more urban. The Sumeritan age began with Nimrod as its leader. Nimrod was the son of Cush. Cush was the son of Ham. Ham was the son of Noah.

As the population grew during the periods of Ubaid 1 and 2, we human beings, again began to move away from our Creator. During this time the first "City" is established. Archeologists now believe that Eridu was the first "city" established in what is called Sumeria in

---

[28] Uruk Period Mesopotamia: The Rise of Sumer (thoughtco.com)

the Mesopotamia region. The findings support that this place was also known as Babylon (Babel).[29] These findings again are consistent with the Bible narrative. We are told of the continual population growth and the development of cities. In Genesis 10 we are told of the first to establish and rule a city, Nimrod, a descendent of Noah's son Ham. Nimrod during this time moved south and founded Eridu, what was called Babel.

Genesis 10:8-10 *"Kush fathered Nimrod, who was the first powerful ruler on earth. He was a mighty hunter before YeHoVaH — this is why people say, "Like Nimrod, a mighty hunter before YeHoVaH." His kingdom began with Babylon, Erekh, Akkad and Kalneh, in the land of Shinar."*

In 1Chronicles 1:10 of the Bible we are also told that Nimrod was the first powerful ruler on earth. Nimrod began his kingdom with the establishment of Eridu (Babel). The development of Eridu is considered the first city in the world by the ancient Sumerians and is among the most ancient of the ruins from Mesopotamia.[30] The

---

[29] Eridu, Sumeria. (ancient-wisdom.com)
[30] https://www.worldhistory.org/eridu

findings at Eridu are consistent with the Biblical narrative as having been established by Nimrod due to its location and archeological findings. As we are told in the Bible, Nimrod established the first "city". Archeologists now believe Nimrod can be identified as Sargon of Akkad developer of the first city.[31]

In Mesopotamia itself the first great king was Nimrod. Research in modern times has enabled us to identify this figure. Some understand Nimrod as Sargon of Akkad, others make an argument that he was Enmerkar, priest-king of Uruk. Both are attributed with founding the first empire on earth. Enmerkar is the first king for whom there is an archaeological record, and, as portrayed on cylinder seals, was a "mighty hunter", just as we are told in the Bible that Nimrod was a "mighty hunter". We can also identify the point in time when the Babel event happened. Right through the fourth millennium Uruk had been growing in size and power, far beyond any other city, and, as in the Genesis account, it was now projecting its power north as far as Nineveh and beyond. It was also justifying its domination theologically. Early on, Mesopotamia had known only one god: Anu, or 'Heaven'. His personal name was Ya, or Ea (sometimes

---

[31] <u>Where was the Tower of Babel? - Dr. Douglas Petrovich - YouTube</u>

written Aya), the same god who was later to introduce himself to the Israelites as Yah/YeHoVaH. But now, people were told, Ea, god of heaven, had transferred his royal power to his daughter Inana, and in sexual union with the king of Uruk, she in turn, had given royal power to the king of Uruk. The myths in effect portrayed her as legitimizing human rule on earth in place of God. Nimrod began this introduction of polytheism, encouraged the people to "make a name for themselves" (Genesis 11) and build the tower that ultimately provoked YeHoVaH to confuse Babel's and the world's language.[32]

As the archeologists continue their work, they find the artifacts and history of Eridu match the Bible account of Nimrod. As we are told in the Bible, Nimrod went on to establish cities throughout what is Southern Mesopotamia. As the archeologists have discovered an empire was built as the Ubaid cultural periods continued and expanded. Settlements were expanding into cities

---

[32] Babel and its after-effects (earthhistory.org.uk)
Douglas Petrovich Where was the Tower of Babel? - Dr. Douglas Petrovich - YouTube Also see:
https://www.academia.edu/5789953/The_Legacies_of_Sargon_and_Joshua_An_Ar chaeological_and_Historiographical_Comparison

and the number of cities increased. The one who lead this development and expansion of this first empire was Nimrod. As we are told in the Bible, Nimrod founded Uruk, Ur, Babylon and the host of cities throughout Shinar, what archeologists call Mesopotamia. And with his wickedness, Nimrod led the people to begin the tower which is known as the Tower of Babel.

This period of history is being documented by archeologists. The more that is discovered, the more truth of the Bible becomes confirmed. All of the evidence, properly understood, interpreted and considered without bias or preset conclusions supports the Biblical narrative.

Nimrod founded Erudu (Babylon) and other areas Uruk, Ur and Kish (Cush) and these were built in the land of Shinar. Nimrod became the leader and became ruler of this area and parts beyond. He was primary instigator of building the tower but more importantly encouraging others to worship other gods, rather than the ONE true GOD YeHoVaH. Again the failure of humankind to obey and follow the commands of YeHoVaH led to destruction. As we are told in the Bible, when the tower (tower of

Babel) in Erudu was constructed the confusion of
language occurred.

Genesis 11:1-9 *"The whole earth used the same
language, the same words. It came about that as they
traveled from the east, they found a plain in the land of
Shinar and lived there. They said to one another, "Come,
let's make bricks and bake them in the fire." So they had
bricks for building-stone and clay for mortar. Then they
said, "Come, let's build ourselves a city with a tower that
has its top reaching up into heaven, so that we can
make a name for ourselves and not be scattered all over
the earth." YeHoVaH came down to see the city and the
tower the people were building. YeHoVaH said, "Look,
the people are united, they all have a single language,
and see what they're starting to do! At this rate, nothing
they set out to accomplish will be impossible for
them! Come, let's go down and confuse their language,
so that they won't understand each other's speech." So
from there YeHoVaH scattered them all over the earth,
and they stopped building the city. For this reason it is
called Babylon [confusion] — because there
YeHoVaH confused the language of the whole earth, and
from there YeHoVaH scattered them all over the earth."*

The archeological evidence which is currently being discovered support what we are told in the Bible. The site Tel Eridu currently known as Abu Shahrain has been identified as the ancient site of Eridu. The findings in chronological order are consistent with the biblical narrative - Founded by the strong leader of the period who introduced the worship of a new god, came to dominate the region, began the building of large temple-Tower of Babel-to new deity which was abandoned, as was the area and surrounding areas were afterwards abandoned. Archeologists have noted these facts.[33]

It has also been noted by the archeological studies that what is known as "the Uruk expansion" began at the time Eridu was abandoned – at the time YeHoVaH confused the Language and spread the peoples out of the areas they had settled before the confusion. Archeological findings indicate a period of rapid decay occurring after the Late Uruk expansion and the rise of the cities throughout the Mesopotamian region.[34] After the

[33] Eridu - Wikipedia,   see also https://www.amazon.com/Nimrod-Archaeology-Tower-Babel-Archaeological-ebook/dp/B07T994VN4 and also Hirst, K. Kris. "Eridu (Iraq): The Earliest City in Mesopotamia and the World." ThoughtCo, Aug. 28, 2020, thoughtco.com/eridu-iraq-earliest-city-in-mesopotamia-170802
[34] Douglas Petrovich Where was the Tower of Babel? - Dr. Douglas Petrovich - YouTube

Confusion of Language, Eridu was abandoned for hundreds of years.[35] This coincided with the Uruk expansion. Archeologists have found the spread of the Uruk and its successor culture Jemdet Nasr spreading from lower Mesopotamia (Shinar) to areas throughout Mesopotamia and beyond. [36] The descendents of Noah continued to spread out across the globe after the Confusion of Language, spreading and developing various cultures as they went. As we are told in the Bible, the sons of Noah and their descendants each spread in different directions, although it must be understood that there was mixing of the various clans from the beginning. Erudu was later reestablished after the 750 years absence caused by the Confusion of Language. The archeological finds indicate that the "Myth" of Erudu's earlier time include the story of the flood, probably from the Atrahasis epic translation by Stephanie Dalley.[37] **Once again we failed to obey YeHoVaH and sought to go our own way**. After the Flood, YeHoVaH instructed us to spread throughout the earth. Rather than obey our Creator, we followed the

---

[35] Where was the Tower of Babel? - Dr. Douglas Petrovich - YouTube

[36] Cultures | Uruk Period (ancientmesopotamia.org)

[37] (Flood texts from Mesopotamia (earthhistory.org.uk)) Hirst, K. Kris. "Eridu (Iraq): The Earliest City in Mesopotamia and the World." ThoughtCo, Aug. 28, 2020, thoughtco.com/eridu-iraq-earliest-city-in-mesopotamia-170802.

words of men as so many even today continue to do. As people followed the ways of Nimrod we moved further and further away from YeHoVaH and righteousness. The human condition for all but the elite worsened, just as the failure to obey YeHoVaH today is resulting in worsening condition for all people. Our failure to love and be loved by our Father is leading to disaster for this world. Our failure to obey YeHoVaH's WORD will result in the destruction of this man made kingdom and its system and everyone who follows it. We are told in the Bible that this will happen and it is happening this very day. Yet, YeHoVaH's love for us is so great that He has provided a Way for those who will take it. Obey Torah and His Commands and trust Yeshua as Messiah and Lord. **It is not too late.**

The cleansing of the flood was to set the next stage of our continuing journey and salvation with Him. But this cleansing was not enough for mankind to grasp the fact that we must love and obey our Creator.

Chapter VII

After the Confusion of Language: The Expansion

The original group of eight grew around the area of Mt. Ararat[38] in present day Turkey where the Ark landed. At this time after the flood, we were given the blessing of YeHoVaH and issued a commandment. We were again given a simple Command; yet again we failed to obey YeHoVaH. We were told to go forth, multiply and populate the whole earth. By the third generation, the group which had grown from the eight moved from the area of Ararat into the plain of Shinar. Instead of obeying, as human beings began to spread into the plains of Shinar a large majority of them choose to stop and began construction of one community.

---

[38] It is currently debated as to whether or not Noah's Ark came to rest on what is currently known as Mt. Ararat. The Bible does say the ark came to rest on **the mountains** of Ararat Genesis 8:4, meaning the area around/near current Mt. Ararat

Genesis 11:1-4"*And the whole earth was of one language and of one speech. And it came to pass, as they journeyed east, that they found a plain in the land of Shinar; and they dwelt there. And they said one to another: 'Come, let us make brick, and burn them thoroughly.' And they had brick for stone, and slime had they for mortar. And they said: 'Come, let us build us a city, and a tower, with its top in heaven, and let us make us a name; lest we be scattered abroad upon the face of the whole earth.'*"

Again mankind failed to obey YeHoVaH. We continued to act in a manner which man determined to act instead of trusting and obeying God. Mankind continued on their path away from YeHoVaH. Man doing as he saw fit, established human rules of conduct. This continued as human beings multiplied. Rather than obey the Command given, human beings decided they would not populate the whole earth but establish a name for themselves and simply stay in their chosen location. Rather than accept the Way of YeHoVaH, we choose our own way and continued and expanded on the governing system which lead to the flood. Men continued to impose their will and dominate other men; a system of behavior establishing that which lead to a governing system led by the first mighty man "Nimrod". He had established the kingdom which was called Babel and continued to grow it even after YeHoVaH confounded the language of all people. YeHoVaH confused the language to prevent humankind from continuing with their plan rather than obeying His Command and coming to know the love of YeHoVaH and His salvation. As when Adam and Eve were put out of the Garden, human beings were not going to be allowed to supplant the plan of GOD. Our Father's love for us is too great. This is His World, we are His creations and we are loved by Him who has given His Son Yeshua as our salvation. We are blessed that the love of our Father is so great for us, He has not forsaken us. His will and plan shall be done.

After the confusion of the language, archeological findings show that people were scattered throughout the region and then the world. As they spread out, the failure to obey God increased. As families enlarged and became tribes, manmade rules and dominance other others expanded. As from the beginning of man's failure to obey God, the strongest among men established dominance, exercising his will over others. As has been shown, each of the established communities continued in the manner of this manmade governing system until this behavior expanded and the first "strong man" emerged, Nimrod.

> **Genesis 10:8-13** *"Cush fathered Nimrod, who was the first powerful ruler on earth. He was a mighty hunter before YeHoVaH—this is why people say, "Like Nimrod, a mighty hunter before YeHoVaH." His kingdom began with the kingdom was Babel, and Erech, and Accad, and Calneh, in the land of Shinar."*

Nimrod's influence and dominance spread throughout the whole world. As Nimrod's rule increased, the further away from YeHoVaH's Word mankind moved. Not only were his manmade rules imposed on all, he introduced new gods which were to be worshipped through him. Archeological evidence has been found in the land of Shinar – the Mesopotamia area, the Fertile Crescent - consistent with the Biblical narrative.[39] The strongest individual established himself as leader and proceeds to do whatever was necessary to control and dominate his community (written in Hebrew, the name "Nimrod" also has the meaning of "rebel" and some say "tyrant"[40]).

---

[39] watchJerusalem September 14, 2018 by Christopher Eames
[40] See Steven Rudd www.bible.ca/nimrod

These actions led ultimately to the desire for control and dominance of the other surrounding communities. Empire building began. Men wanted to continue their displacement of the one true GOD with gods they made of and for themselves.

Nimrod in the Shinar Valley region established the first manmade kingdom. Mankind chose to allow themselves to be ruled by men rather than trust and obey God. The use of violence resulted in the communities accepting, yielding, all power to the "leaders". Order was desired over perceived chaos so giving up innate desire for freedom occurred for a period of time. Nimrod was the first to use these conditions as ruler of the first empire to arise from the Shinar region. Archaeological evidence has been discovered in the area of Shinar consistent with these accounts. Ancient Sumerian tablets tell the story of the "mighty hunter" who ruled over the territory of Mesopotamia which includes the areas of Babel to Ninevah as described in the Book of Genesis.[41] Nimrod established his "rule" consistent with that "rule" introduced by Cain-the use of force. Continuing his conquests of other families surrounding Babel, his

---

[41] See "Babel and its after-effects" A New Approach to World History
www.earthhistory.org.uk

empire arose to include - Shinar, Chaldea, Elam, Karrak, Accad and Babel. Shinar expanded as the people spread out; although, the kingdoms of Nimrod did weakened and went into decline after the confusion of language and people left the immediate area of the Tower of Babel.

After the confounding of the language, people spread out. Ashur eventually formed and ruled early Assyria.

Genesis 10:8-13"... "Like Nimrod, a mighty hunter before YeHoVaH." His kingdom began with the kingdom was Babel, and Erech, and Accad, and Calneh, in the land of Shinar." Out of that land went forth Asshur, and builded Nineveh, and Rehobothir, and Calah, and Resen between Nineveh and Calah—the same is the great city."

These developed into empires of Shinar, Chaldea, Elam, Karrak, Accad, Babel, the Neo-Assyrian Empire, Egypt, later Assyria, and Babylonia. Interestingly archeologist have discovered evidence of two groups living in this area with almost identical customs but two distinct

languages, Sumerian and Akkadian - additional evidence
of the Great Flood and the Confusion of Language.[42]

All these manmade kingdoms followed the governing
pattern begun by Cain and brought to full force by
Nimrod. Each new ruler would, to establish his
dominance over the people, conquer again for himself all
the people who had been subjected to the ruler ship
before him. He needed to conquer for himself the very
people of the area to which he had succeeded, and which
his predecessor, often his own father, had conquered. As
the desire to rule over larger and larger masses of area,
the desire to create and rule over "empire", spread, the
use of the conquer/re-conquer method spread. Each
new ruler believing it necessary, not only that each
succeeding ruler should conquer anew to himself the
very people who had been conquered by the previous
ruler, often times his own father, but he himself, to
maintain his dominion, was compelled to conquer and
conquer again, annually the very same people during the
entire time of his reign. The use to the violence on
communities, forcing compliance and acceptance of men
as rulers and false gods became the accepted way.
People became submissive, yielding all power to the

"leaders". Order was desired over chaos so giving up innate desire for freedom occurred. The desire/spirit of/for freedom was not completely driven out of the population. Continual subjugation was and continued to be needed.[43]

It was also at this time after the Confusion of Language that the Bronze Age as designated by archeologists began. The emergence of elites is one thing that characterizes the onset of the Early Bronze Age. The previously egalitarian social order was shattered, replaced by totalitarian regimes in which the majorities were subservient to a ruler and his associates. As the descendents of Noah spread out over the world taking with them the practices of Nimrod, similarly, the rise of civilization in Egypt and China were essentially stories of kings who claimed to have divine authority to rule and thereby channeled the resources of society so that they themselves received glory, wealth and power. But in reality they usurped God; they had established a kingdom where man reigned.[44]

---

[43] See "The Empires of the Bible from the Confusion of Tongues to the Babylonian Captivity" by Alonzo Trevier Jones

[44] Babel and its after-effects (earthhistory.org.uk)

Chapter VIII

The Development of Nations

After the Confusion of Language, the descendants of Noah left the area of Babel and from the other areas they had settled and spread out. As they went forth reinforcing the settlements that had been established and established new ones, they spread the false beliefs encouraged by Nimrod and multiple gods were made up and worshipped. All peoples knew God exists and there is in fact God. They incorporated what they had learned from Noah and combined that with the false beliefs propounded by Nimrod and incorporated new beliefs as they went along to new places. This explains why all the worlds' current religions mirror each other to a great extent. The basics were taken from Noah and perverted.

With the confounding of language, migration began in earnest. In the Torah, Genesis 9:18 we are told that the whole earth was populated by the son's of Noah - Shem,

Ham and Japheth. Genesis 10 tells us the genealogy of the sons and the basic areas settled by each of them.

Japheth

Genesis 10:2-5 "The sons of Japheth were Gomer, Magog, Madai, Yavan, Tuval, Meshekh and Tiras. The sons of Gomer were Ashkenaz, Rifat and Togarmah. The sons of Yavan were Elishah, Tarshish, Kittim and Dodanim. From these the islands of the nations were divided into their lands, each according to its language, according to their families, in their nations."

Japheth's descendants, who had stayed closest to the original settlement in Thamanin, moved west into Anatolia (Turkey), Greece, Central and Greater Asia. Japheth's descendants are traceable to the Aryan people of Europe, Iran and north India. The descendants of Japheth also went north of Thamanin towards the Caucus Mountains. The migration included the areas beyond the Caucus Mountains north into the slavic countries, west into what is Europe as far as France and east to Asia through China and Japan. According to the first century historian Josephus the descendants of Japheth also populated the areas around the Taurus and

Amanus mountains, living in Asia as far as the river
Tansis and also inhabiting Europe to Cadiz.[45] Gomer and
his sons are said to have lived in the land of Franza by
the rivers Franza and Senah, an area which included
modern France and Belgium area.[46] Gomer's
descendants are believed to have migrated as far west as
current day Wales and east as far as China arriving at the
Foot of current day Russia.

As we are told in the Bible, Noah cultivated a grape
vineyard upon settling in the Ararak area. His skill in
this area was passed along. One of Japheth's sons
descendants, Kartlos, from whom the Kartvelian people
arose (current day Georgians) developed this skill. Some
of the earliest evidence of grape cultivation and wine
making has been discovered among the artifacts of the
Kartvelians.[47] The descendants of Japheth primarily
(along with some of the descendants of Ham and Shem
as the clans had already intermixed some) continued to
establish settlements as they went into Anatolia, north
Mediterranean and Central and Western Europe and into
Asia. Japheth and his descendants are believed to have

---

[45] (Antiquities of the Jews, Book 1, Chapter 6),
[46] The War of Gog of Magog Concerning Turkey and Libya - Time of Reckoning
Ministry
[47] https://en.wikipedia.org/wiki/Georgians

settled in areas around the Black and Caspian Seas, the Greek islands (Aegean Sea Region), as well as the islands of Cyprus, Crete and Rhodes.[48]

Ham

Genesis 10: 6-20 *"The sons of Ham were Cush, Mizraim, Put, and Canaan. The sons of Cush were S'va, Havilah, Savta, Ra'mah and Savt'kha. The sons of Ra'mah were Sh'va and D'dan. Cush fathered Nimrod, who was the first powerful ruler on earth. He was a mighty hunter before YeHoVaH — this is why people say, "Like Nimrod, a mighty hunter before YeHoVaH." His kingdom began with Bavel (Babylon), Erekh, Akkad and Kalneh, in the land of Shinar. Ashur went out from that land and built Ninveh, the city Rechovot, Kelach, and Resen between Ninveh and Kelach — that one is the great city. Egypt was the father of the Ludites, Anamites, Lehabites, Naphtuhites, Pathrusites, Kasluhites (from whom the Philistines came) and Caphtorites. Canaan was the father of Sidon his firstborn, and of the Hittites, Jebusites, Amorites, Girgashites, Hivites, Arkites , Sinites, Arvadites, Zemarites and Hamathites. Later the Canaanite clans scattered and the borders of*

Canaan reached from Sidon toward Gerar as far as Gaza, and then toward Sodom, Gomorrah, Admah and Zeboyim, as far as Lasha. These are the sons of Ham by their clans and languages, in their territories and nations."

As we are told in Torah, Genesis 10 et seq the sons of Ham migrated to, and then after the Confusion of Language, from the Shinar region, which Nimrod had come to command, to the Eastern/Southern Mediterranean Sea area, current day Egypt, a portion of Arabia, Northern and throughout Africa. Some of these descendants as they rounded the Persian Gulf area are thought to have travels westward by sea, arriving in the Central America region which explains the pyramid structures found in this area.[49] As they went forth the communities were named after the founder or their relative. Ham's son Canaan settled the lands on the eastern shore of the Mediterranean, according to Genesis 10:19 these are the Canaanites. They were also later known as the Phoenicians.[50] These grandchildren of

[49] See "The African presence in Ancient America by Ivan Van Sertima; Olmec Origins: The Mystery of Mexico's Megalith Builders - Hugh Newman - YouTube; work of S.C. Compton

[50] See "Nimrod and Egypt's Forgotten Origins" by Peter Goodgame Nimrod and Egypt's Forgotten Origins (hope-of-israel.org)

Ham, include the Hittites who also migrated to Anatolia and the Sinites who migrated to Asia including China and Japan and Polynesia.[51] The Canaanite clans borders reached from Sidon toward Gerar as far as Gaza, and then toward Sodom, Gomorrah, Admah and Zeboyim, as far as Lasha. The people of Egypt are direct descendants of Mizraim[52]. Ludim was a son of Mizraim and is believed to be those that settled to the west of Egypt, perhaps farther than any other Mizraite tribe. Lud and the Ludim are mentioned in four passages of the prophets -- (Isaiah 66:19; Jeremiah 46:9; Ezekiel 27:10; 38:5) There is little doubt that the son of Mizraim is the one nation intended in these passages and the preponderance of evidence is in favor of the Mizaraite Ludim [53]. Descendents of Mizraim were also the Kasluchim fathers of the Philistines.

Shem

Genesis 10:21-32 "Children were also born to Shem, ancestor of all the descendants of 'Eber and older brother of Japheth. The sons of Shem were Elam, and

---

[51] Sinites (Nation) – Four Corner Ministries (4CM)
[52] See Amazing Bible Timeline Mizraim - Mizraim – Amazing Bible Timeline with World History
[53] See The Bible Hub Ludim - Topical Bible: Ludim (biblehub.com)

Asshur, and Arpachshad, and Lud, and Aram." And the sons of Aram: Uz, and Hul, and Gether, and Mash. And Arpachshad begot Shelah; and Shelah begot Eber. And unto Eber were born two sons; the name of the one was Peleg; for in his days was the earth divided; and his brother's name was Joktan. And Joktan begot Almodad, and Sheleph, and Hazarmaveth, and Jerah; and Hadoram, and Uzal, and Diklah; and Obal, and Abimael, and Sheba; and Ophir, and Havilah, and Jobab; all these were the sons of Joktan. And their dwelling was from Mesha, as thou goest toward Sephar, unto the mountain of the east. These are the sons of Shem, after their families, after their tongues, in their lands. These are the clans of Noah's sons, according to their lines of descent, within their nations. From these the nations spread out over the earth after the flood."

The descendants of Shem had migrated from Thamanin down into Shinar and from there, went into Arabia and to the Far East. These descendents settled in the areas of southern Mesopotamia, including what some believe to be the establishment of Asshur that became early Assyria and the body of the Arabian Peninsula and also into Asia. (Genesis 10:11) We are told in the Bible that the sons of Eber were of primary importance among

Shem's descendants. Eber's son Joktan and his sons are believed to have migrated east into Asia.[54] The descendants of Ebers other son Peleg, established communities, which included the establishment Haran, the location from which Abraham, from which the Messiah can be traced, is from. As each of these communities grew, conflict between them increased. Each utilized the governing system established and brought forth by Nimrod.

As mankind spread throughout the earth, YeHoVaH's love for us continued. YeHoVaH created the means for us to come back to Him and into His love by creating a people through which He would reintroduce Himself to mankind. He demonstrated this love by providing for us a blessing. It was through the decedents of Shem that (this blessing was delivered to us) we receive this blessing of YeHoVaH.

---

[54] ORIENTAL ORIGINS IN THE BIBLE (eifiles.cn)

Chapter IX

YeHoVaH's Blessing

After the descendants of Noah had spread across the earth, implementing and further developing the various systems of governance based upon that of Nimrod, in His love for us, YeHoVaH went forth with His plan to reintroduce Himself to human kind and provide our way back to Him through His salvation. He did this by creating a group of people to which His Word was given to be spread throughout the world and through which His Son, Yeshua, would come as our salvation. Many generations after the Confusion of Language, after the descendents of Shem were established in the area of Ur near Babylon, Abram was born and later moved to Haran in current southeast Turkey. Through this man Abram, YeHoVaH would create His people through which He would bring the offer of salvation back to the world.

The Bible tells us that Abram was called by YeHoVaH to leave his father's house and begin what is to be our salvation.

Genesis 12:1-9 *""Now YeHoVaH said unto Abram: 'Get thee out of thy country, and from thy kindred, and from thy father's house, unto the land that I will show thee. And I will make of thee a great nation, and I will bless thee, and make thy name great; and be thou a blessing. And I will bless them that bless thee, and him that curseth thee will I curse; and in thee shall all the families of the earth be blessed." 'So Abram went, as YeHoVaH had spoken unto him; and Lot went with him; and Abram was seventy and five years old when he departed out of Haran. And Abram took Sarai his wife, and Lot his brother's son, and all their substance that they had gathered, and the souls that they had gotten in Haran; and they went forth to go into the land of Canaan; and into the land of Canaan they came. And Abram passed through the land unto the place of Shechem, unto the terebinth of Moreh. And the Canaanite was then in the land. And YeHoVaH appeared unto Abram, and said: 'Unto thy seed will I give this land'; and he builded there an altar unto YeHoVaH, who appeared unto him. And he removed from thence unto the mountain on the east of Beth-el, and pitched his tent, having Beth-el on the west, and Ai on the east; and he builded there an altar unto YeHoVaH, and called upon the name of YeHoVaH. And Abram journeyed, going on still toward the South."*

And with this the creation of the people through which YeHoVaH's salvation is offered to all who will take it, began. Abram continued to obey YeHoVaH and continued his sojourn throughout the area of Canaan. To insure the newly formed families' survival, to escape a famine, Abram took his family into Egypt after which he left Egypt with many riches. A while later after leaving Egypt, Abram again was called by YeHoVaH.

Genesis 13:14-18 *""And YeHoVaH said unto Abram, after that Lot was separated from him: 'Lift up now thine eyes, and look from the place where thou art, northward and southward and eastward and westward; for all the land which thou seest, to thee will I give it, and to thy seed for ever. And I will make thy seed as the dust of the earth; so that if a man can number the dust of the earth, then shall thy seed also be numbered. Arise, walk through the land in the length of it and in the breadth of it, for unto thee will I* *give it.' And Abram moved his tent, and came and dwelt by the terebinths of Mamre, which are in Hebron, and built there an altar unto YeHoVaH."*

YeHoVaH continued His blessing of Abram, assuring the blessing that is for the entire world for those that will receive it. After Lot had been captured in a raid into Sodom where Lot had gone to live after separating from Abram, YeHoVaH enabled Abram to take a small group of men and defeat the raiders and rescuing those of Sodom. (Genesis 14) After this YeHoVaH came again to Abram.

Genesis 15:1-21 *""Some time later the word of YeHoVaH came to Abram in a vision: "Don't be afraid, Abram. I am your protector; your reward will be very great." Abram replied, "YeHoVaH, God, what good will your gifts be to me if I continue childless; and Eli'ezer from Dammesek inherits my possessions? You haven't given me a child," Abram continued, "so someone born in my house will be my heir." But the WORD of YeHoVaH came to him: "This man will not be your heir. No, your heir will be a child from your own body." Then He brought him outside and said, "Look up at the sky, and count the stars — if you can count them!*

Your descendants will be that many!" He believed in YeHoVaH, and He credited it to him as righteousness. Then He said to him, "I am YeHoVaH, who brought you out from Ur-Kasdim to give you this land as your possession." He replied, "YeHoVaH, God, how am I to know that I will possess it?" He answered him, "Bring me a three-year-old cow, a three-year-old female goat, a three-year-old ram, a dove and a young pigeon." He brought Him all these, cut the animals in two and placed the pieces opposite each other; but he didn't cut the birds in half. Birds of prey swooped down on the carcasses, but Abram drove them away. As the sun was about to set, a deep sleep fell on Abram; horror and great darkness came over him. YeHoVaH said to Abram, "Know this for certain: your descendants will be foreigners in a land that is not theirs. They will be slaves and held in oppression there four hundred years. But I will also judge that nation, the one that makes them slaves. Afterwards, they will leave with many possessions. As for you, you will join your ancestors in peace and be buried at a good old age. Only in the fourth generation will your descendants come back here, because only then will the Emori be ripe for punishment." After the sun had set and there was thick darkness, a smoking fire pot and a flaming torch appeared which passed between these animal parts. That day YeHoVaH made a covenant with Abram: "I have given this land to your descendants — from the Vadi of Egypt to the great river, the Euphrates River — the Kenite, and the Kenizzite, and the Kadmonite, and the Hittite, and the Perizzite, and the Rephaim, and the Amorite, and the Canaanite, and the Girgashite, and the Jebusite.""

Abram continue living in the land of Canaan with his wife Sarai. Having no children yet as YeHoVaH had promised, Sarai suggested Abram who was 86 years old at the time, father a child with Sarai's Egyptian servant girl. Abram did so.

When Abram was 99, YeHoVaH again appeared to him.

Genesis 17:1-8 *" When Abram was 99 years old YeHoVaH appeared to Abram and said to him, "I am El Shaddai [God Almighty]. Walk in My presence and be pure-hearted. I will make My covenant between Me and you, and I will increase your numbers greatly." Abram fell on his face, and God continued speaking with him: "As for Me, this is My covenant with you: you will* *be the father of many nations. Your name will no longer be Abram [exalted father], but your name will be Abraham [father of many], because I have made you the father of many nations. I will cause you to be very fruitful. I will make nations of you, kings will descend from you. "I am establishing My covenant between Me and you, along with your descendants after you, generation after generation, as an everlasting covenant, to be God for you and for your descendants after you. I will give you and your descendants after you the land in which you are now foreigners, all the land of Canaan, as a permanent possession; and I will be their God.""*

Continuing

Genesis 17:15-22 *"God said to Abraham, "As for Sarai your wife, you are not to call her Sarai [mockery]; her name is to be Sarah [princess]. I will bless her; moreover, I will give you a son by her. Truly I will bless her: she will be a mother of nations; kings of peoples will come from her." At this Abraham fell on his face and laughed — he thought to himself, "Will a child be born to a man a hundred years old? Will Sarah give birth at ninety?" Abraham said to God, "If only Ishmael could* *live in your presence!" God answered, "No, but Sarah your wife will bear you a son, and you are to call him Isaac [Yitz'chak-laughter]. I will establish my covenant with him as an everlasting covenant for his descendants after him. But as for Ishmael, I have heard you. I have blessed him. I will make him fruitful and give him many descendants. He will father twelve princes, and I will make him a great nation. But I will establish my covenant with Isaac, whom Sarah will bear to you at this time next year." With that, God finished speaking with Abraham and went up from him"*

The child YeHoVaH promised Abraham was born when Abraham was 100 years old. This child, Isaac, later fathered Jacob, who afterwards was given the name Israel by YeHoVaH (Genesis 32:28) and went on to father twelve sons. These twelve sons became the twelve tribes of Israel.

YeHoVaH loves us and His WORD is truth.

As YeHoVaH had told Abraham, his decedents, the twelve tribes of Israel went into Egypt where they eventually became slaves. After four hundred years YeHoVaH had Moses lead the children of Israel out of bondage and out of Egypt into the land He had promised Abraham.

YeHoVaH's WORD tells us how Israel went into Egypt, their trials there and their leaving by the Mighty Hand of YeHoVaH. We are told how the Mighty Hand of YeHoVaH brought plagues on Egypt, demonstrating the power of YeHoVaH and convincing the Egyptians they could not disobey YeHoVaH and that they must free Israel. We are told of the travels of Israel from Egypt to the Promised Land and the works of YeHoVaH bringing His chosen ones, the ones through whom He is reintroduced to mankind and His Son Yeshua, our salvation, home.

The truth of what we are told in the Bible is continually being verified. Archeological findings verify what we are told in the Bible.[55] We must trust in Him and what He has told us, it will happen. YeHoVaH has told us the fate of this world in and through His WORD. We are in the last days. As we are told in Isaiah 55:6, "Seek

---

[55] Top 10 Artifacts Show Biblical Exodus was Real History | Israel (patternsofevidence.com)

YeHoVaH while He is available, call on Him while He is still nearby." The time is short.

As YeHoVaH brought Israel to the Promised Land, He took them to Mount Sinai located in current day Saudi Arabia where He gave the Israelites His WORD which is for all humankind. In these, YeHoVaH gave us the manner and way we are supposed to live our lives with each other on this earth. As He has from the beginning of His creation He has provided us the way in which to live. But again we fail to listen to Him and seek to go our own way. He has told us this will result in disaster and it will.

When Israel established itself in the Promised Land, they had been told that they needed to follow what YeHoVaH had given them through His WORD. Through the first five books of the Bible, the Torah (Torah is used by some to incorporate the entire WORD of YeHoVaH as in itself the word Torah can mean "teachings", "law" or "commands"), we are given the Commands of YeHoVaH we are to follow. Israel then, just as we today, failed to obey the WORD of YeHoVaH. Through the Torah and the words of the Prophets and Writings and now the Gospel

Record, we are told that the man made system humankind has decided to follow will be destroyed.

YeHoVaH's WORD is His blessing to us. In His WORD His Son Yeshua is included. The love, the blessing of YeHoVaH is for the whole world.

Chapter X

Trust His WORD

One of the ways YeHoVaH shows us He is the ONLY GOD and that His WORD is truth is by telling us of things that will happen before they occur. No other so-called god does this. Through the truth of the words of the prophets we can be confident that the WORD of YeHoVaH is true. We have been told of the Rise of the Last Beast Kingdom and the results by the prophet Daniel. Our failure to obey Torah and the Commands of YeHoVaH and trust that His Son Yeshua is Messiah and Lord will result in the complete destruction of this man made system and the annihilation of most people living today – 2022 AD. YeHoVaH's love has provided a WAY for those who will take it, however.

At the end of the forty years after YeHoVaH had spoken at Mount Sinai, as they were about to enter the Promised Land, Moses told the people of Israel what YeHoVaH demanded when they entered their new home. Through

Deuteronomy 27 – 31, Israel is told they must obey the Torah and the Commands of YeHoVaH. They are told of the blessings and the curses, what they could expect with obedience and what they could expect if they failed to obey the Torah and Commands of YeHoVaH.

Deuteronomy 27:-9-10 *"Next Moshe and the cohanim, who are L'vi'im, spoke to all Israel. They said, "Be quiet; and listen, Israel! Today you have become the people of YeHoVaH your God. Therefore you are to listen to what YeHoVaH your God says and obey His mitzvot and laws, which I am giving you today."*

Deuteronomy 28:1-2 *"If you listen closely to what YeHoVaH your God says, observing and obeying all His mitzvot which I am giving you today, YeHoVaH your God will raise you high above all the nations on earth; and all the following blessings will be yours in abundance — if you will do what YeHoVaH your God says:*

Deuteronomy 28: 15 *"But if you refuse to pay attention to what YeHoVaH your God says, and do not observe and obey all His mitzvot and regulations which I am giving you today, then all the following curses will be yours in abundance:*

Deuteronomy 28:-58-59 *"If you will not observe and obey all the words of this Torah that are written in this book, so that you will fear this glorious and awesome name, YeHoVaH your God; then YeHoVaH will strike down you and your descendants with extraordinary plagues and severe sicknesses that go on and on..."*

Continuing

Deuteronomy 28:63-65 *"Thus it will come about that just as once YeHoVaH took joy in seeking to do you good and increase your numbers, so now YeHoVaH will take joy in causing you to perish and be destroyed, and you will be plucked off the land you are entering in order to take possession of it. YeHoVaH will scatter you among all peoples from one end of the earth to the other, and there you will serve other gods, made of wood and stone, which neither you nor your ancestors have known. Among these nations you will not find repose, and there will be no rest for the sole of your foot; rather YeHoVaH will give you there anguish of heart, dimness of eyes and apathy of spirit.*

When Israel failed to listen and obey Torah and the Commands of YeHoVaH they lost the Promised Land and were disbursed across the world. YeHoVaH told them this would happen and it did. YeHoVaH's love for us is so great, that He has always provided a way back to Him for those who will chose it. In our time we have Torah and He has given us Yeshua, His Son, as our means back to Him. Trust and Obey the WORDS of YeHoVaH. HalleluYah!!!

YeHoVaH has used His prophets to continually warn and tell the leadership and the people of Israel that their failure to listen to and obey the Commands of YeHoVaH would result in their losing what YeHoVaH had given them. The loss of Israel and the Temple are examples. After the building of the Temple in Jerusalem by Solomon, Israel is told that we must love YeHoVaH and show this love by obeying Torah and His Commands.

2 Chronicles 7:15-22 "*Now My eyes will be open and My ears will pay attention to the prayer made in this place. For now I have chosen and consecrated this house, so that My name can be there forever; My eyes and heart will always be there. As for you, if you will live*

Just as YeHoVaH had foretold when Israel failed to obey
Torah and the Commandments, they lost both Israel and
the Temple. It began with the division of Israel into two
kingdoms, the Northern Kingdom, Israel and the

Southern Kingdom, Judah as Solomon failed to continue to obey Torah and the Commandments. YeHoVaH used the prophet Achiyah to tell of this coming division of Israel. Ahiyah was from Shiloh.

***1 Kings 11:29-40** "... Achiyah was wearing a new cloak, and the two of them were alone in open country. Achiyah took hold of his new cloak that he was wearing and tore it into twelve pieces. Then he said to Jeroboam, "Take ten pieces for yourself! For here is what YeHoVaH the God of Israel says: 'I am going to tear the kingdom out of Solomon's hand, and I will give ten tribes to you. But he will keep one tribe for the sake of My servant David and for the sake of Jerusalem, the city I have chosen from all the tribes of Israel. I will do this because they have abandoned Me and worshipped 'Ashtoret the goddess of the Tzidoni, K'mosh the god of Mo'av and Milkom the god of the people of 'Amon. They haven't lived according to My ways, so that they could do what was right in My view and obey My regulations and rulings, as did David his father. Nevertheless, I will not take the entire kingdom away from him; but I will make him prince as long as he lives, for the sake of David My servant, whom I chose, because he* *obeyed My mitzvot and regulations. However, I will take the kingdom away from his son and give ten tribes of it to you. To his son I will give one tribe, so that David My servant will always have a light burning before Me in Jerusalem, the city I chose for Myself as the place to put My name. I will take you, and you will rule over everything you want; you will be king over Israel. Now if you will listen to all that I order you, live according to My ways and do what is right in My view, so that you observe My regulations and mitzvot, as David My servant did; then I will be with you, and I will build you a lasting dynasty, as I built for David; and I will give Israel to you. For this [offense] I will trouble David's descendants, but not forever." Because of this Solomon tried to kill Jeroboam; but Jeroboam roused himself, fled to Egypt, to Shishak king of Egypt, and stayed in Egypt until the death of Solomon."*

Jeroboam did become king of Israel but he too failed to obey Torah and the Commands of YeHoVaH. He led Israel to the worship of other gods and their failure to obey Torah and the Commands of YeHoVaH. YeHoVaH said unto Jeroboam's wife:

***1 Kings 14: 7**-16 ""Go, tell Jeroboam that this is what YeHoVaH, the God of Israel, says: 'I raised you up from among the people and appointed you ruler over My people Israel. I tore the kingdom away from the house of David and gave it to you, but you have not been like My servant David, who kept My commands and followed Me with all his heart, doing only what was right in My eyes. You have done more evil than all who lived before you. You have made for yourself other gods, idols made of metal; you have aroused My anger and turned your back on Me. "'Because of this, I am going to bring disaster on the house of Jeroboam. I will cut off from Jeroboam every last male in Israel—slave or free. I will burn up the house of Jeroboam as one burns dung, until it is all gone. Dogs will eat those belonging to Jeroboam who die in the city, and the birds will feed on those who die in the country. YeHoVaH has spoken!' "As for you, go back home. When you set foot in your city, the boy will die. All Israel will mourn for him and bury him. He is the only one belonging to Jeroboam who will be buried, because he is the only one in the house of Jeroboam in whom YeHoVaH, the God of Israel, has found anything good."YeHoVaH will raise up for himself a king over Israel who will cut off the family of Jeroboam. Even* *now this is beginning to happen. And YeHoVaH will strike Israel, so that it will be like a reed swaying in the water. He will uproot Israel from this good land that He gave to their ancestors and scatter them beyond the Euphrates River, because they aroused YeHoVaH's anger by making Asherah poles. And He will give Israel up because of the sins Jeroboam has committed and has caused Israel to commit.""*

This evil continued in Israel from one ruler to the next as each refused to obey Torah and the Commands of YeHoVaH. The truth of YeHoVaH's WORD was then seen as the tribes of the Northern Kingdom of Israel were devastated, captured and carried away by Shalmaneser V.

***2 Kings 18:9-12** "" It was in the fourth year of King Hizkiyahu, which was the seventh year of Hoshea son of Elah, king of Israel, that Shalmaneser king of Ashur advanced against Shomron and laid siege to it. At the end of three years they captured it — that is, Shomron was captured in the sixth year of Hizkiyahu, which was the ninth year of Hoshea king* *of Israel. The king of Ashur carried Israel away captive to Ashur and settled them in Halach, in Havor on the Gozan River and in the cities of the Medes. <u>This happened because they did not heed the voice of **YeHoVaH** their God, but violated His covenant, everything that Moses the servant of **YeHoVaH** had ordered them to do, and would neither hear it nor do it.</u>"(Emphasis added)*

At the time of the destruction of the Northern Kingdom of Israel, the king of the Southern Kingdom Judah was Hezekiah.

__2 Kings 18:1-8__ ""In the third year of Hoshea son of Elah king of Israel, Hezekiah son of Ahaz king of Judah began to reign. He was twenty-five years old when he became king, and he reigned in Jerusalem twenty-nine years. His mother's name was Abijah daughter of Zechariah. He did what was right in the eyes of YeHoVaH, just as his father David had done. He removed the high places, smashed the sacred stones and cut down the Asherah poles. He broke into pieces the bronze snake Moses had made, for up to that time the

Israelites had been burning incense to it. (It was called Nehushtan.) Hezekiah trusted in YeHoVaH, the God of Israel. There was no one like him among all the kings of Judah, either before him or after him. He held fast to YeHoVaH and did not stop following Him; he kept the commands YeHoVaH had given Moses. And YeHoVaH was with him; he was successful in whatever he undertook. He rebelled against the king of Assyria and did not serve him. From watchtower to fortified city, he defeated the Philistines, as far as Gaza and its territory."

Unfortunately for those of Judah, the kings that followed Hezekiah did not do as he did, obeying Torah and the Commands of YeHoVaH. After the destruction of the Northern Kingdom of Israel, YeHoVaH sent prophets to the Southern Kingdom of Judah to remind and warn those remaining Israelites of the need to obey Torah and the Commands of YeHoVaH. Jeremiah was one of these prophets:

Jeremiah 1:18-19 *"For today, you see, I have made you into a fortified city, a pillar of iron, a wall of* *bronze against the whole land —against the kings of Judah, against its princes, against its cohanim and the people of the land. They will fight against you, but they will not overcome you, for I am with you," says YeHoVaH, "to rescue you.""*

After the death of Hezekiah, his son Manasseh began his rule of Israel's Southern Kingdom Judah. He did not follow the ways of his father Hezekiah in obeying Torah and the Commands of YeHoVaH.

***2 Kings 21:2-6** "He did what was evil from YeHoVaH's perspective, following the disgusting practices of the nations whom YeHoVaH had expelled ahead of the people of Israel. For he rebuilt the high places Hezekiah his father had destroyed; he erected altars for Ba'al and made an asherah, as had Ach'av king of Israel; and he worshipped all the army of heaven and served them. He erected altars in the house of YeHoVaH, about which YeHoVaH had said, "In Jerusalem I will put My name." He erected altars for all the army of heaven in the two courtyards of the house of YeHoVaH. He made his son pass through the fire* *[as a sacrifice]. He practiced soothsaying and divination and appointed mediums and persons who used spirit guides. He did much that was evil from YeHoVaH's perspective, thus provoking Him to anger."*

YeHoVaH had Jeremiah warn the people of Judah.

Jeremiah 17:-19-27 *"Then YeHoVaH said this to me: "Go, and stand at the People's Gate, where the kings of Judah go in and out, and at all the gates of Jerusalem; and say to them: 'Kings of Judah, all Judah and all living in Jerusalem who enter through these gates, hear the word of YeHoVaH! Here is what YeHoVaH says: "If you value your lives, don't carry anything on Shabbat or bring it in through the gates of Jerusalem; don't carry anything out of your houses on Shabbat; and don't do any work. Instead, make Shabbat a holy day. I ordered your ancestors to do this, but they neither listened nor paid attention; rather, they stiffened their necks, so that they wouldn't have to hear or receive instruction. However, if you will pay careful heed to me," says YeHoVaH "and carry nothing through the*

*gates of this city on Shabbat, but instead
make Shabbat a day which is holy and not for doing
work; then kings and princes occupying the throne
of David will enter through the gates of this city,
riding in chariots and on horses. They, their princes,
the people of Judah and the inhabitants of Jerusalem
will enter; and this city will be inhabited
forever. They will come from the cities of Judah,
from the places surrounding Jerusalem, from the
land of Benjamin, from the Sh'felah, from the hills
and from the Negev, bringing burnt offerings,
sacrifices, grain offerings, frankincense and
thanksgiving sacrifices to the house
of YeHoVaH. But if you will not obey me and
make Shabbat a holy day and not carry loads
through the gates of Jerusalem on Shabbat, then I
will set its gates on fire; it will burn up the palaces of
Jerusalem and not be quenched."'"*

After Judah continued its failure to obey Torah and the
Commands of YeHoVaH under Hezekiah's son Manasseh
a further warning was given.

Jeremiah18:11-12 *"So now, tell the people of Judah and those living in Jerusalem that this is what YeHoVaH says: 'I am designing disaster for you, working out My plan against you. Turn, each of you, from his evil ways; improve your conduct and actions.' "But they will answer, 'It's hopeless! We will stick to our own plans; each of us will stubbornly follow his own evil desires!'"*

As the people of Judah continued to follow their leaders and failed to obey the WORD of YeHoVaH, Our Father's love for us caused Him to reach out to us with more warnings and telling of the consequence of failing to obey His WORD.

2 Kings 21:10-16 *"YeHoVaH spoke this message through His servants the prophets: "Because Manasseh king of Judah has done these disgusting things; because he has done things more wicked than anything the Emori, who were there before him, did; also because with his idols he made Judah sin; therefore here is what YeHoVaH the God of Israel, says: 'I am going to bring such calamity on Jerusalem and Judah that the ears of all who hear of it will tingle. I will measure Jerusalem with the same measuring cord that I used over Shomron, the same plumbline as for the house of Ach'av. I will scour Jerusalem clean just as one scours a plate, scouring it and then turning it upside down. I will abandon the remnant of My heritage, delivering them into the power of their enemies — they will become prey and plunder for all their enemies; because they have done what is evil from My perspective and have provoked Me to anger from the day their ancestors came out of Egypt to this very day.'" Moreover, Manasseh shed so much innocent blood that he flooded Jerusalem from one end to the other — this in addition to his sin through which he caused Judah to sin by doing what is evil from YeHoVaH's perspective."*

Evil continued in Judah after Manasseh as he was succeeded by his son Amon.

2 Kings 21:19-22 *"Amon was twenty-two years old when he began his reign, and he ruled for two years in Jerusalem. His mother's name was Meshulemet the daughter of Harutz from Yotvah. He did what*

*was evil from YeHoVaH's perspective, as had
Manasseh his father. He followed entirely the
manner of life of his father, serving the idols that his
father served and worshipping them. He abandoned
YeHoVaH, the God of his ancestors, and did not live
in YeHoVaH's way. After Amon was killed, the people
of Judah made Josiah his son king in place of him."*

As Jeremiah continued to serve YeHoVaH during the time
of King Josiah, the Southern Kingdom of Judah was again
told of the Torah and the Commands of YeHoVaH as the
WORD of YeHoVaH was found in the Temple built by
Solomon. Already with a heart for YeHoVaH, Josiah had
sent word to have restoration work done on the Temple.
As this was being done, the Torah was found among the
things of the Temple. News of the discovery was taken to
Josiah.

2 Kings 22:10-20 *"Shafan the secretary also told
the king, "Hilkiyah the cohen hagadol gave me a
scroll." Then Shafan read it aloud before the king.
" When the king heard the words of the Book of the
Law, he tore his robes. He gave these orders to
Hilkiah the priest, Ahikam son of Shaphan, Akbor*

son of Micaiah, Shaphan the secretary and Asaiah the king's attendant: "Go and inquire of YeHoVaH for me and for the people and for all Judah about what is written in this book that has been found. Great is YeHoVaH's anger that burns against us because those who have gone before us have not obeyed the words of this book; they have not acted in accordance with all that is written there concerning us." Hilkiah the priest, Ahikam, Akbor, Shaphan and Asaiah went to speak to the prophet Huldah, who was the wife of Shallum son of Tikvah, the son of Harhas, keeper of the wardrobe. She lived in Jerusalem, in the New Quarter. She said to them, "This is what YeHoVaH, the God of Israel, says: Tell the man who sent you to Me, 'This is what YeHoVaH says: I am going to bring disaster on this place and its people, according to everything written in the book the king of Judah has read. Because they have forsaken Me and burned incense to other gods and aroused My anger by all the idols their hands have made, My anger will burn against this place and will not be quenched.' Tell the king of Judah, who sent you to inquire of YeHoVaH, 'This is what YeHoVaH, the God of Israel, says concerning the words you heard: Because your heart was responsive and you humbled yourself *before YeHoVaH when you heard what I have spoken against this place and its people—that they would become a curse and be laid waste—and because you tore your robes and wept in My presence, I also have heard you, declares YeHoVaH. Therefore I will gather you to your ancestors, and you will be buried in peace. Your eyes will not see all the disaster I am going to bring on this place.'" So they took her answer back to the king."*

After this word of YeHoVaH was received by Josiah, King Josiah then read the WORD of YeHoVaH to the priest and people of Jerusalem/Judah and ordered the high priest, the priests next in rank and the doorkeepers to remove from the temple of the YeHoVaH all the articles made for the false gods and the worship thereof. King Josiah also got rid of the mediums and spiritists, the household gods, the idols and all the other detestable things seen in Judah and Jerusalem. Just as he had done at Bethel, Josiah removed all the shrines at the high places that the kings of Israel had built in the towns of Samaria and that had aroused YeHoVaH's anger. Josiah slaughtered all the priests of those high places on the altars and burned human bones on them.

This fulfilled the prophecy given to Jeroboam when Israel was taken from Him, again confirming the truth of YeHoVaH's WORD. (1 Kings 12:2)

King Josiah then went back to Jerusalem ordered all the people to "Celebrate the Passover to YeHoVaH their God", as it is written in the WORD of YeHoVaH. Neither in the days of the judges who led Israel nor in the days of the kings of Israel and the kings of Judah had any such Passover been observed. But in the eighteenth year of King Josiah, this Passover was celebrated to YeHoVaH in Jerusalem. King Josiah did all he could to fulfill the requirements of the law written in the book that Hilkiah the priest had discovered in the temple of YeHoVaH. Neither before nor after King Josiah was there a king like him who turned to YeHoVaH as he did—with all his heart and with all his soul and with all his strength, in accordance with all the Law of Moses.

After the death of Josiah, his son ruled in Judah.

2 Kings 23:31-37 "Jehoahaz was twenty-three years old when he began his reign, and he ruled for three months in Jerusalem. His mother's name was Hamutal the daughter of Jeremiah from Livnah. He did what was evil from YeHoVaH's perspective, following the example of everything his ancestors had done. Pharaoh N'khoh imprisoned him at Rivlah in the land of Hamat, so that he would not be able to rule in Jerusalem. He also imposed a penalty on the land of three-and-a-quarter tons of silver and sixty-six pounds of gold. Then Pharaoh N'khoh made Elyakim the son of Josiah king in place of Josiah his father and changed his name to Jehoiakim. He also carried Jehoahaz off to Egypt, where he died. Jehoiakim remitted the silver and gold to Pharaoh; but in order to pay the money Pharaoh demanded, he had to levy a tax on the land. He taxed the people of the land, each according to his means, to pay the silver and gold to Pharaoh N'khoh. Jehoiakim was twenty-five years old when he began his reign, and he ruled for eleven years in Jerusalem. His mother's name was Z'vudah the daughter of Pedaiah, from Rumah. He did what was evil from the perspective of YeHoVaH, following the example of everything his ancestors had done."

Even after the dedicated work of Josiah in his attempt to take the people of Judah back to YeHoVaH and after his death, Jeremiah's continuous reminders of what had happened to the Northern Kingdom of Israel because they failed to obey Torah and follow the Commands of YeHoVaH (just as we today ignore YeHoVaH and fail to obey His Torah even though He sent us His Son Yeshua to remind us to obey Torah and the Commands of YeHoVaH-see Matthew 5:17-21 and Matthew 7:21-24), the people of Judah did not turn from their evil ways.

YeHoVaH then did as He said He would. Again, YeHoVaH told what He was going to do before He did it. He had the message delivered by Jeremiah.

Jeremiah 27:1-11 *"At the beginning of the reign of Jehoiakim the son of Josiah, king of Judah, this word came to Jeremiah from YeHoVaH: "YeHoVaH says this to me: 'Make yourself a yoke of straps and crossbars, and put it on your neck. Send [similar yokes] to the kings of Edom, of Moab, of the people of 'Amon, of Tyre, and of Zidon by means of the envoys they send to Jerusalem, and to Zedekiah king of Judah. Give them this message for their masters by telling their envoys that YeHoVaH -Tzva'ot, the God of Israel, says for them to tell their masters: """I made the earth, humankind, and the animals on the earth by My great power and My outstretched arm; and I give it to whom it seems right to Me. For now, I have given over all these lands to My servant Nebuchadnezzar the king of Babylon; I have also given him the wild animals to serve him. All the nations will serve him, his son and his grandson, until his own country gets its turn — at which time many nations and great kings will make him their slave. The nation and kingdom that refuses to serve this Nebuchadnezzar king of Babylon, that will not put their necks under the yoke of the king of Babylon, I will punish," says YeHoVaH "with sword, famine and plague, until I have put an end to them through him. ""You, therefore, don't listen to your prophets, diviners, dreamers, magicians or sorcerers, when they tell you that you won't be subject to the king of Babylon; for they are prophesying lies to you that will result in your being removed far from your land, with My driving you out, so that you perish. But the nation that puts its neck under the yoke of the king of Babylon and serves him, that nation I will allow to remain on their own soil," says YeHoVaH. "They will farm it and live there.""*

The WORD of YeHoVaH is TRUTH. History itself shows this. YeHoVaH tells that which will happen and it does.

It was during the time of Jehoiakim's (Y'hoyakim) ruler ship of Judah that YeHoVaH allowed the kingdom of Judah to be taken by Nebuchadnezzar (2 Kings 24:1). We are told in the Bible that this would happen and it did happen. We are told in the Bible that it did happen and this fact has been established by archeological findings throughout history[56]

2 Kings 24:1-16 "*It was in Jehoiakim's time that Nebuchadnezzar king of Babylon invaded. Jehoiakim became his vassal for three years, but then he turned against him and rebelled. YeHoVaH sent against him raiding parties from the Kasdim, Aram, Moab and the people of 'Amon; He sent them against Judah to destroy it, in keeping with the word of YeHoVaH which He had spoken through His servants the prophets. Yes, it was at YeHoVaH's order that this happened to Judah, in order to remove them from His sight because of the sins of Manasseh and all he had done, and also because of the innocent blood he had*

---

[56] <u>Ancient tablets reveal life of Jews in Nebuchadnezzar's Babylon | Reuters</u>

shed — for he had flooded Jerusalem with innocent blood, and YeHoVaH was unwilling to pardon. Now the rest of the acts of Jehoiakim, and all that he did, are they not written in the book of the chronicles of the kings of Judah? Then Jehoiakim slept with his ancestors, and Jehoiachin his son took his place as king. And the king of Egypt came not again any more out of his land; for the king of Babylon had taken, from the Brook of Egypt unto the river Euphrates, all that pertained to the king of Egypt. Jehoiachin was eighteen years old when he began his reign, and he ruled in Jerusalem for three months. His mother's name was Nehushta the daughter of Elnathan, from Jerusalem. He did what was evil from YeHoVaH's perspective, following the example of everything his father had done. It was then that the officers of Nebuchadnezzar king of Babylon marched on Jerusalem and laid siege to the city. Nebuchadnezzar king of Babylon himself went to the city while it was under siege; and Jehoiachin king of Judah went out to meet the king of Babylon — he, his mother, and his servants, princes and officers; and the king of Babylon took him captive in the eighth year of his reign. He also carried away from there all the treasures in the house of YeHoVaH and the treasures in the royal palace.

He cut in pieces all the articles of gold which Solomon king of Israel had made in the temple of YeHoVaH, as YeHoVaH had said would happen. He carried all Jerusalem away captive — all the princes, all the bravest soldiers — 10,000 captives; also all the craftsmen and metalworkers. No one was left but the poorest people of the land. Jehoiachin he carried off to Babylon; likewise he carried off the king's mother, the king's wives, his officers and the main leaders of the land from Jerusalem into captivity in Babylon. All the strong men — 7,000 of them, as well as 1,000 craftsmen and metalsmiths, all of them strong and trained for war — the king of Babylon brought captive to Babylon."

YeHoVaH's WORD is true. He told Israel, both the Northern and Southern Kingdoms, what the consequences would be of their failure to obey Torah and His Commands. They did not follow the WORD of YeHoVaH and what He told them would happen, did happen. YeHoVaH's WORD is true and what He has told to us for our time, this time in the twenty-first century, will also happen. The man made systems which rule this world are going to be destroyed.

YeHoVaH's love for us is so great however, that even with the continual failure to obey Torah and His Commands He is willing to forgive and has provided us a way back to Him. Well before the exile to Babylon, at the time of the building of the Temple by Solomon He tells us:

> ***2 Chronicals 7:12-14*** *"YeHoVaH appeared to Solomon by night and said to him, "I have heard your prayer and have chosen this place for Myself as a house of sacrifice. If I shut up the sky, so that there is no rain; or if I order locusts to devour the land; or if I send an epidemic of sickness among My people; then, if My people, who bear My name, will humble themselves, pray, seek My face and turn from their evil ways, I will hear from heaven, forgive their sin and heal their land."*

The WORD of YeHoVaH is true and our failure to listen and follow YeHoVaH will result in our destruction. Just as Israel was told of its destruction for failing to obey Torah and the Commands of YeHoVaH, our failure to obey Torah, obey His Commands and trust Yeshua as

Messiah and Lord will result in the destruction of the man made systems under which the world currently operates. This destruction will take place.

YeHoVaH loves us and has provided the way back for those who will follow and obey. We MUST listen. Hear His cry for us. Obey Torah, obey His Commands and trust Yeshua as Messiah and Lord and know His salvation. Only those that do will know His salvation. The man made systems will be ending soon. There is no rapture as the church wrongly teaches. Do not trust the words of any man. TRUST the WORD of YeHoVaH as He has given it to us. Read His WORD yourself and ask YeHoVaH to have His Holy Spirit guide you so that you may know its truth. He has always told us of His willingness to forgive. He uses His WORD through His prophets to show us the way.

In the Book of Joel He tells us:

> *Joel 2:12-14 "Yet even now," says YeHoVaH "turn to Me with all your heart, with fasting, weeping and lamenting." Tear your heart, not your garments;*

and turn to YeHoVaH your God. For He is merciful and compassionate, slow to anger, rich in grace, and willing to change His mind about disaster. Who knows? He may turn, change His mind and leave a blessing behind Him, [enough for] grain offerings and drink offerings to present to YeHoVaH your God."

Trust YeHoVaH always.

Chapter XI

Foretelling of the Beasts Kingdoms

After the conquest of the Southern Kingdom of Israel by Nebuchadnezzar, the vast majority of the people of Judah were taken into Babylon. It was at this time that YeHoVaH tells of the future of humankind. He tells us of the coming of the beast kingdoms run by manmade systems that will rule at various times leading up to the last beast kingdom and its ultimate destruction by YeHoVaH and the salvation of those who have loved and followed Him. We are told of these things throughout His WORD in the Book of Daniel, the Psalms, the Prophets and the Gospel Record.

The description of the coming kingdoms (run by manmade systems) is laid out in the Book of Daniel. Daniel was one of those from Judah who was taken into Babylon after the conquest by Nebuchadnezzar. Daniel's love for YeHoVaH resulted in God giving him knowledge and skill in all learning and wisdom; and an understanding in all visions and dreams (Daniel 1:17). With these abilities given to Daniel, Daniel was used to tell us of the coming kingdoms, the manmade governing bodies which would dominate the world.

Sometime after his captivity in Babylon, Daniel became aware of a dream which the ruler of Babylon, Nebuchadnezzar, had which terrified Nebuchadnezzar. Nebuchadnezzar called upon the wise men and seers in his kingdom and demanded that they provide him with an explanation for this dream. As not to be provided with a false or misleading response to his demand, Nebuchadnezzar refused to tell the wise men and seers the content of the dream. When none of them were able to respond as Nebuchadnezzar had requested, he ordered all of them killed. Upon learning of this decree, Daniel asked for time that he might be able to provide the proper response. Daniel and three other Israelites, who had been taken with him to the king's court, prayed and asked YeHoVaH to provide the answer Nebuchadnezzar was looking for. God answered Daniel and the other young men's prayer by showing Daniel what Nebuchadnezzar had demanded. Daniel asked for and was granted an audience with king Nebuchadnezzar:

Daniel 2:24-49 *"So Daniel went to see Arioch, whom the king had charged with destroying the sages of Babylon, and said to him, "Don't destroy the sages of Babylon! Bring me before the king, and I will give the king the interpretation." Quickly Arioch brought Daniel before the king and told him, "I have found one of the exiles of Judah who will reveal the interpretation to his majesty." The king said to Daniel (Daniel had been renamed Belt'shatzar by the Babylonians), "Can you tell me what I dreamt and what it means?" Daniel answered the king, "No sage, exorcist, magician or astrologer can tell his majesty the secret he has asked about. But there is a God in heaven who unlocks mysteries, and He has revealed to King Nebuchadnezzar what will happen in the end of days. Here are your dream and the visions you had in your head when you were in bed.*

"Your majesty, when you were in bed, you began thinking about what would take place in the future; and He who reveals secrets has revealed to you what will happen. Yet this secret has not been revealed to me because I am wiser than anyone living, but so that the meaning can be made known to your majesty, and then you can understand the thoughts of your own mind.

"Your majesty had a vision of a statue, very large and extremely bright; it stood in front of you and its appearance was terrifying. The head of the statue was of fine gold, its chest and arms of silver, its trunk and thighs of bronze, its legs of iron, and its feet partly of iron and partly of clay. As you watched, a stone separated itself without any human hand, struck the statue on its feet made of iron and clay, and broke them in pieces. Then the iron, the clay, the bronze, the silver and the gold were all broken into pieces which became like the chaff on a threshing-floor in summer; the wind blew them away without leaving a trace. But the stone which had struck the statue grew into a huge mountain that filled the whole earth.

"That is what you dreamt, and now we will give the king its interpretation. Your majesty, king of kings, to whom the God of heaven has given the kingdom, the power, the strength and the glory; so that wherever people, wild animals or birds in the air live, He has handed them over to you and enabled you to rule them all — you are the head of gold. But after you another kingdom will rise, inferior to you; then a third kingdom, of bronze, which will rule the whole world. The fourth kingdom will be as strong as iron. Iron can break anything into pieces, pulverize it and *crush it. So just as iron can crush anything, this kingdom will break the other kingdoms into pieces and crush them. Finally, you saw the feet and toes made partly of pottery clay and partly of iron; this will be a divided kingdom; yet it will have some of the firmness of iron, since you saw the iron mixed with clay from the ground. Just as the toes of the feet were part iron and part clay, this kingdom will be partly strong and partly brittle. You saw the iron mixed with clay; that means that they will cement their alliances by intermarriages; but they won't stick together any more than iron blends with clay.*

"In the days of those kings the God of heaven will establish a kingdom that will never be destroyed, and that kingdom will not pass into the hands of another people. It will break to pieces and consume all those kingdoms; but it, itself, will stand forever — like the stone you saw, which, without human hands, separated itself from the mountain and broke to pieces the iron, the bronze, the clay, the silver and the gold. The great God has revealed to the king what will come about in the future. The dream is true, and its interpretation is reliable."

Then King Nebuchadnezzar fell on his face and worshipped Daniel; he ordered that a grain offering and incense be offered to him. To Daniel the king said, "Your God is indeed the God of gods, the Lord of kings and a revealer of secrets, since you have been able to reveal this secret." The king promoted Daniel to a high rank, gave him many rich gifts and made him governor of the entire province of Babylon and head of all the sages of Babylon. At Daniel's request, the king put Shadrach, Meshach, and Abed-nego, the three young men who had prayed with Daniel, in charge of the affairs of the province of Babylon, while Daniel remained in attendance on the king."

YeHoVaH enabled Daniel to tell Nebuchadnezzar what he had dreamt and the meaning of the dream, saving the life of Daniel and his fellow Judanian companions **AND** YeHoVaH told us of the kingdoms with manmade governing systems which were to and have come into being. Daniel went on to serve Nebuchadnezzar and several other Babylonian kings as one of the highest ranking officials in Babylon until the end of his life. Daniel also had other visions which explained what these other manmade ruling systems would do and consists of.

Chapter XII

The Beast Kingdoms

The first kingdom which Daniel identified was that of king Nebuchadnezzar, Babylon. Prior to its ruler ship, Babylon was under the control of the Assyrian Empire. Sometime after Assyria had taken control of and dispersed the Northern Kingdom of Israel, Babylon overtook the Assyrians and became the dominate power in the world.[57] In addition to the vision which Daniel had and told to Nebuchadnezzar, Babylon's position was shown to Daniel in other visions. In Daniel 7, Daniel saw four beasts rise from the sea, each different from the other. Daniel was told in his dream, again, that each beast represented a kingdom which would rein on earth. The first as shown to Daniel by YeHoVaH was Babylon and was represented by a lion. The next was represented by a bear which was told to devour much flesh. In accordance with the statute seen by Nebuchadnezzar, this would be the silver kingdom which followed Babylon. The next looked like a leopard with

---

[57] Babylonian Empire - Livius

wings and four heads and was given dominion on earth. Accordingly, this is the bronze portion of the statute. In keeping with Daniel's interpretation of Nebuchadnezzar's dream, the last beast was the most terrifying, with iron teeth and 10 horns after which another horn arose and plucked three of the previous horns.

Historically each of the first three kingdoms arose and fell as indicated in the Bible. In the fourth generation after Nebuchadnezzar, the Babylonian empire was toppled. The Bible stated that this would occur prior to its occurrence in Jeremiah 25:12 and Jeremiah 50. Babylon was overtaken by the Persians. The vast majority of Israel was still in Babylon and the geographic Israel was still in tatters. After Israel had been exiled in Babylon for seventy years, as told in Isaiah, Cyrus of Persia authorized the rebuilding of the Temple in Jerusalem and released the Israelites and they returned to Jerusalem and reestablished Israel and rebuilt the Temple in Jerusalem (Isaiah 44 and Isaiah 45). After the Babylonian kingdom of Nebuchadnezzar, the Medes/Persian Empire arose. Eventually Cyrus became ruler, conquered and took control of Babylon. The Medes/Persians were ultimately defeated by the Greeks.

We are told of this in the Bible before it occurred in Daniel 8 when Daniel tells of his vision of a Ram which was dominant in the world until a Goat destroyed the Ram and established its dominance over the world (Daniel 8). The Greek empire as told in the Bible dominated the world until it split after its initial and greatest ruler Alexander the Great died. The Greek culture continued to dominate the separated parts of the empire and continued until they were defeated by the Romans. The Greek culture continued within the new Roman Empire and was adopted and merged into Roman culture. This Greek/Roman culture eventually became the dominant culture in the world. This Roman Empire dominated the world for centuries.   This Roman Empire expanded and contracted over the centuries. At one point for a considerable time period, the Persian Empire reemerged in the eastern portion of this empire. This Greek/Roman Empire through a series of wars has been reconstituted and the Greek/Roman culture/empire still dominates the world to this day. The last beast spoken of by Daniel is here today - The Greek/Roman Empire is morphing into the terrifying beast Daniels describes.

The last beast kingdom told to us by Daniel is here today. It is an outgrowth of the third beast and is establishing itself to take the form which will dominate and control the world in the manner told to us in the Bible. Our world has come to be dominated by groups which have no interest in following our Creator YeHoVaH and obeying His Torah and Commandments. There is a war against God and His creation. We are told that this will be the case during the time of the end, the period immediately before YeHoVaH makes His existence and His salvation known to all people.

Since the day of the Confusion of Language mankind has continued to move further and further away from YeHoVaH, establishing manmade governing systems by which small group of elites dominate and dictate to the rest, the manner in which they are to live. As people moved from the land where Noah and his family came to rest after the Flood to places across the earth, these governing systems have been set up. The same basic model has been used throughout the earth. Rather than obeying YeHoVaH and seeking to be with and rely on Him, those seeking control, using the system established by Nimrod set themselves up as leaders, representing a made up god, who would provide for the people the things needed for everyday existence. This took varied forms across the world. Chiefs were established who appointed priests who appointed over seers who enforced the demand for production of items required to be given to the elites who would then dole out subsistence to the masses who they demanded loyalty and obedience from. On every continent these manmade systems arose. Rather than rely and call upon YeHoVaH for that which is needed, humankind followed the calling of Nimrod to rely on those like him to provide the things needed.

The system which dominates the world today is a continuation of this system with the addition of the thing which has made it so powerful, **money**. Again we have continued to fail to call upon our Creator. As groups of people became larger and the type of items changed from things that can be easily exchanged, the use of money came to dominate the exchange of goods. We have gone from societies which paid taxes in the form of crops to the elite and exchanging eggs for milk at the market to societies which use money for the exchange of all things. As money increased in its usage, the elites then began to accumulate money and use money itself as a means to generate more money which would require more people to produce things which created more money. This was the beginning of capitalism.

From its inception capitalism was a means to control the masses, a method used to convince those subjugated to the ruling class to believe that the system would take care of their need, preventing those being ruled from challenging those in control of whatever governing system was in place. Capitalism was that system put in place to prevent humankind from reaching out to God and falsely presenting the world as mans salvation. Prior to any market based economy, rulership of each group was based on a hierarchy from king on down to worker. Each was dependent on the one above it for their needs. The king would claim a special relationship with the god created for that particular group giving him the power to rule/dictate. The king would allocate resources to those under him and demand from them tribute for his upkeep and falsely claiming he provided for those under him. Each group would duplicate this process on down to the worker who had no one under him and would begin production of goods which went up the chain ultimately to the king. When money replaced goods as the primary means of exchange, money/capital itself began to be used to produce more money. This required more workers to make more goods. As the number of people increased, it was necessary to provide for these people as to keep pressured from the top, so money and the means to make it were made available to a different class of workers. The use of money in this way has expanded in various ways to all corners of the globe enabling control of the masses. Money was and still is said to be that which will take care of all problems. This helps to take people further from God who loves them. Instead of bringing people closer to our Creator, it takes people away with the delusion that man and his worldly goods can take care of himself instead of relying on YeHoVaH as we are suppose to.

The capitalistic beast system does all it can to replace YeHoVaH with the god of money. It creates a false worldly paradise, devoid of the principles of justice and righteousness we are called to seek by God. It has produced scientific creations - what it likes to calls advancements – that enable it to claim there is no God and as Nimrod encouraged all, no need to rely on God-YeHoVaH- as human beings could rely on other gods, currently money, to do all things for themselves. As we humans proclaimed when building the Tower of Babel, "let's build ourselves a city with a tower that has its top reaching up into heaven, so that we can make a name for ourselves" (Genesis 11:4). The current beast system has convinced the vast majority of people that this is the way we should live, forsaking God or at least not having to concern ourselves with Him, simply being a "good person" giving to charity occasionally, observing man made rituals like christmas and easter or other religious observances created by the other man made religions and sitting in the manmade religious ceremonies each week. This is the power of this capitalistic system. As Yeshua tells us in Revelation, people will declare, "who can fight the beast" Revelation 13:4.

Further proof that the capitalistic system is not from God is the method used to fuel the system. Capitalism requires the exchange of money from buyer to seller. The sellers have devised ways of motivating the buyers to spend money. This method is advertising. Sellers present products as "needs" regardless as to the utility of the product. In doing this, appeals to human being's carnal nature are continual. The very thing we are told in the WORD of God to put behind us, our carnal selves, is the very thing that capitalism promotes and demands. The advertising used to attract buyers in the capitalistic system rely on sexual references, jealousy, envy, that which makes us feel special or sets us apart, and/or any emotion which makes us act in our own interest – selfish ambition. These are the very things we are told NOT to seek, yet are called to seek them every day by the beast system which pulls us away from God (See Galatians 5:19-16).

We have moved further from our Father at this point in time than at any point in human history. We began to pull away at the very beginning in the Garden when we could not obey ONE simple command. But YeHoVaH's love for us is so great, He has continually reached out to us, calling us back. YeHoVaH called Israel back through the prophets. He has given us His Son Yeshua as our salvation, a means to come back to Him. He is reaching out to us one last time. We can turn back even now. Let us repent and turn back to our Father.

The expansion of mankind has seen various ways to motivate people to do what the elites need done to generate what those of the elite want, control and power. Money is that motivator which has worked the best for them. The type of political ruling body does not matter. Be it communism, fascism, democracy, all that is important to the elite is to have the masses do what they want. Money has become the ultimate in efficiency to do this. The money based system has made the movement into the last beast kingdom possible. The power and type of control needed to crush all things exists with this system. Just as we are told in the Bible, this kingdom will have the power to break the other kingdoms into pieces and crush them (Daniel 2:40). We see how in our day, the year 2021, the money based system has enabled the Greek/Roman empire to break all other empires, dictatorial kings, the fascist, the communist, first the Russians, and now even China has turned to a money based system to control its people and China will be among the ten kingdoms which will rule when the antichrist rules over this world.

The composition, stature and the destruction which the last beast will inflict is also told to us in Daniel 7. Daniel describes this last beast as follows:

Daniel 7:19-25" *"Then I wanted to know what the fourth beast meant, the one that was different from all the others, so very terrifying, with iron teeth and bronze nails, which devoured, crushed and stamped its feet on what was left; and what the ten horns on its head meant; and the other horn which sprang up and before which three fell, the horn that had eyes and a mouth speaking arrogantly and seemed greater than the others. I watched, and that horn made war with the holy ones and was winning, until the Ancient One came, judgment was given in favor of the holy ones of the Most High, and the time came for the holy ones to take over the kingdom. This is what he said: 'The fourth animal will be a fourth kingdom on earth. It will be different from the other kingdoms; it will devour the whole earth, trample it down and crush it. As for the ten horns, out of this kingdom ten kings will arise; and yet another will arise after them. Now he will be different from the earlier ones, and he will put down three kings. He will speak words against the Most High and try to exhaust the holy ones of the Most High. He will attempt to alter the seasons and the law; and [the holy ones] will be handed over to him for a time, times and half a time...."*

The world in which we live in today in the twenty first century is perfectly set up to and has already shown the characteristics of the last beast. The mechanisms for destruction have become so sophisticated that mankind has the ability to physically destroy any designated point on our planet earth. Also, our failure to look to YeHoVaH and live in the manner He has laid out for us in the Bible has resulted in the catastrophes which are destroying the atmosphere, polluting the oceans with manmade plastics and chemicals and watching as famines, fires and storms destroy the places we live. The rise of dictatorships across the globe is happening now. Even the manmade creation of "democracy" is being turned into a dictatorship of the wealthy elite who do nothing in those so called democracies but put in place laws and restrictions to control its people and increase the wealth of the elite. Those countries which do not pretend and are lead by strongmen use physical force and money to control their people and provide for their elites.

The system and the circumstances which will create the ruling ten horns of the last beast are here and taking place now. After World War I, the countries of the world attempted in their own strength to create world peace and formed the League of Nations. This lasted until a short time later World War II broke out engulfing the whole world once again. After millions of souls were lost during this war period, an attempt was made again to bring the world together in peace with the formation of the United Nations. Once again, we failed to reach out to our Father and do as He would have us do.

The formation of the United Nations has not stopped wars from being raged. Wars taking various forms continue. Global conflict is increasing every day. China is now insisting on a position of power in the world and demanding recognition of its right to rule what it perceives as its part of the world. Russia seeks to regain its perceived power. The Muslim nations and Islamic culture around the world continue their attempt to destroy current day Israel and take a leadership position. The United States and its Christians attempt to maintain their position of dominance with its use of money and false belief that they are following God. These factors will result in another major global war. We are told of this war. It will take place shortly at the time of the Day of YeHoVaH. In Daniel 7, Zechariah 12-14, and Revelation this war is told to us - this war which will result in the destruction of this last beast kingdom.

Daniel 7:26-27" *But when the court goes into session, he will be stripped of his rulership, which will be consumed and completely destroyed. Then the kingdom, the rulership and the greatness of the kingdoms under the whole heaven will be given to the holy people of the Most High. Their kingdom is an everlasting kingdom, and all rulers will serve and obey them.'"*

There is hope for those that will trust and obey. Trust
YeHoVaH.

God, YeHoVaH, loves His people. God wants and seeks all
people. All those who obey Torah, His Commands and
trust Yeshua as Messiah will be saved. Please join. His
love is beyond measure.

Chapter XIII

The Last Days

In Daniel 8 we are told of the consolidation of power under the last beast kingdom. An earthly ruler will emerge which will bring together the various factions throughout the world under his leadership (Daniel 8:9 and 8:23-26). Daniel is told that this vision is of the time of the end. This "time of the end" is the period preceding the return of YeHoVaH with His Son Yeshua.

In December 2021 our world was in the midst of a global pandemic having killed over five million people since its start in December 2019 and still killing an average of over 7000 people per day. The United States is in a political quagmire that has not been seen since its Civil War in the mid 1800's when the nation divided. An actual coup attempt was made by the former president who was defeated in the 2020 election on January 6, 2021. The forces behind that insurrection are still active and planning a means to either again divide the country or institute "laws" and means to control the population to serve the interest of the elites. In Europe, groups seeking to take control of the populous by either force or imposition of "laws" stressing "security" are on the rise. In Asia China has morphed into a dictatorial capitalistic society controlling its population through force and money and seeking to dominate the entire Asian Pacific region. In the Middle East, forces continue in their efforts to eliminate Israel and are increasingly supported by more and different groups in this effort. These factors will eventually coalesce, an earthly leader will emerge and the last beast kingdom described by Daniel will come into full force before bringing about the end of the manmade kingdoms/systems and the destruction of this world as it is known today.

Further proofs of the truth of the Bible are the words written by Peter. Peter is one of the disciples of Yeshua. Yeshua is the ONLY Messiah who died and rose again, providing salvation for ALL who will obey Torah and the Commands of YeHoVaH and trust that Yeshua is Messiah. Peter tells us:

__2 Peter 3:1-7__ "Dear friends, I am writing you now this second letter; and in both letters I am trying to arouse you to wholesome thinking by means of reminders; so that you will keep in mind the predictions of the holy prophets and the command given by the Lord and Deliverer through your emissaries. First, understand this: during the Last Days, scoffers will come, following their own desires and asking, "Where is this promised 'coming' of his? For our fathers have died, and everything goes on just as it has since the beginning of creation." But, wanting so much to be right about this, they overlook the fact that it was by God's Word that long ago there were heavens, and there was land which arose out of water and existed between the waters, and that by means of these things the world of that time was flooded with water and destroyed. It is by that same WORD that the present heavens and earth, having been preserved, are being kept for fire until the Day of Judgment, when ungodly people will be destroyed."

We are in the period of the Last Days. Scoffers go about mockingly claiming there is no truth in the Bible. Even many of those who claim to follow Jesus and/or believe in God, hold only that the Bible is only a moral code or writings by people that provide a philosophy to help guide ones way. The manmade kingdoms take care of all problems and that god is not something needed or to be believed in. Human beings fail to obey Torah and the Commands of God. People alter the creations made by God-YeHoVaH-even going so far as to use science to manipulate and physically change people themselves. Most people do not heed the warnings and trust the WORD of YeHoVaH. All those who fail to trust YeHoVaH do so at their peril. There is only ONE God, YeHoVaH, God of Israel and Father of Yeshua; YeHoVaH is Creator of ALL things. He tells us through His WORD that this world and its manmade governing systems are going to be destroyed and how this destruction will take place. We are in the period of the last beast told to us by Daniel and the Book of Revelation.

As we continue to live in this period when the last beast is forming, we observe another factor and thing that we are told will happen before the world comes together against YeHoVaH and destruction comes upon all people who fail to obey Torah and the Commands of YeHoVaH and this world. We are told in the Bible that the people of this world will continually reject God by rejecting His

teachings/Commandments and His people Israel.
(Reading the Bible and asking that the Holy Spirit of God
guide and lead you through its Words will bring you to
the understanding that YeHoVaH's – God's - people are
those who obey Torah and the Commandments of
YeHoVaH and trust Yeshua as Messiah.) We are told of
this rejection in Psalm 2:

*Psalm 2:1-3" Why are the nations in an uproar, the
peoples grumbling in vain? The earth's kings are taking
positions, leaders conspiring together, against YeHoVaH
and His anointed. They cry, "Let's break their fetters!
Let's throw off their chains!"*

This psalm tells of mankind's continual rebellion against
God. God is in charge though and continuing in this
psalm tells us so and of the destruction of the manmade
system. He also tells us how to avoid this fate.

*Psalm 2:4-12"He who sits in heaven laughs;
YeHoVaH looks at them in derision. Then in His anger
He rebukes them, terrifies them in His fury. "I Myself
have installed My king on Zion, My holy mountain." "I
will proclaim the decree: YeHoVaH said to Me, 'You are
My son; today I became your father. Ask of Me, and I will*

make the nations your inheritance; the whole wide world will be your possession. You will break them with an iron rod, shatter them like a clay pot.'" Therefore, kings, be wise; be warned, you judges of the earth. Serve YeHoVaH with fear; rejoice, but with trembling. Kiss the Son, lest He be angry, and you perish along the way, when suddenly His anger blazes. How blessed are all who take refuge in Him."

Psalm 2:12 "How blessed are ALL who take refuge in Him" - Our means of protection during the coming destruction. HalleluYah!!!

God's WORD is truth. He has told us of the last beast kingdom and it is coming into form now and will occur. YeHoVaH has provided warnings to us in the past and given us opportunities to turn back to Him to avoid coming disaster, but we failed to listen. In Jeremiah 7, well before the destruction of the Temple and disbursement of the people of Judah and Jerusalem, God tells the people that their continual sinning would result in the destruction of the Temple and the displacement of those who lived there.

Jeremiah 7:1-15 *"This word came to Jeremiah from YeHoVaH: "Stand at the gate of the house of YeHoVaH and proclaim this word: 'Listen to the word of YeHoVaH, all you from Judah who enter these gates to worship YeHoVaH! Here is what YeHoVaH -Tzva'ot, the God of Israel, says: "Improve your ways and actions, and I will let you stay in this place. Don't rely on that deceitful slogan, 'The temple of YeHoVaH, the temple of YeHoVaH — these [buildings] are the temple of YeHoVaH.' No, but if you really improve your ways and actions; if you really administer justice between people; if you stop oppressing foreigners, orphans and widows; if you stop shedding innocent blood in this place; and if you stop following other gods, to your own harm; then I will let you stay in this place, in the land I gave to your ancestors forever and ever. Look! You are relying on deceitful words that can't do you any good. First you steal, murder, commit adultery, swear falsely, offer to Ba'al and go after other gods that you haven't known. Then you come and stand before Me in this house that bears My name and say, 'We are saved' — so that you can go on doing these abominations! Do you regard this house, which bears My name, as a cave for bandits? I can see for Myself what's going on," says YeHoVaH. "Go to the place in Shiloh that used to be Mine, that used to bear My name, and see what I did to* *it because of the wickedness of My people Israel. I spoke to you again and again, but you wouldn't listen. I called you, but you wouldn't answer. Now," says YeHoVaH, "because you have done all these things, I will do to the house that bears My name, on which you rely, and to the place I gave you and your ancestors, what I did to Shiloh; and I will drive you out of My presence, just as I drove out all your kinsmen, all the descendants of Efrayim."*

YeHoVaH reminds those of Judah and Jerusalem what happened to their brethren in Israel who failed to obey Torah and His Commands.

Continuing in Jeremiah 7 –

Jeremiah 7:16-34 *" "So you, don't pray for this people! Don't cry, pray or intercede on their behalf with Me; because I won't listen to you. Don't you see what they are doing in the cities of Judah and in the streets of Jerusalem? The children gather the wood, the fathers light the fire, and the women knead the dough to make cakes for the queen of heaven; and, just to provoke Me,* *they pour out drink offerings to other gods! Are they really provoking Me," asks YeHoVaH, "or are they provoking themselves, to their own ruin?" Therefore, here is what YeHoVaH Elohim says: "My anger and fury will be poured out on this place, on men, animals, trees in the fields and produce growing from the ground; and it will burn without being quenched." Thus says YeHoVaH-Tzva'ot, the God of Israel: "You may as well eat the meat of your burnt offerings along with that of your sacrifices. For I didn't speak to your ancestors or give them orders concerning burnt offerings or sacrifices when I brought them out of the land of Egypt. Rather, what I did order them was this: 'Pay attention to what I say. Then I will be your God, and you will be My people. In everything, live according to the way that I order you, so that things will go well for you.' But they neither listened nor paid attention, but lived according to their own plans, in the stubbornness of their evil hearts, thus going backward and not forward. You have done this from the day your ancestors came out of Egypt until today. Even though I sent you all My servants the prophets, sending them time after time, they would not listen or pay attention to Me, but stiffened their necks; they did worse than their ancestors. So tell them all this; but they won't listen to*

*you; likewise, call to them; but they won't answer
you. Therefore, say to them:*

*'This is the nation that has not listened to the voice of
YeHoVaH their God. They won't take correction;
faithfulness has perished; it has vanished from their
mouths. Cut off your hair, and throw it away, take up a
lament on the bare hills, for YeHoVaH has rejected and
abandoned the generation that rouses His anger.'*

*"For the people of Judah have done what is evil from My
perspective," says YeHoVaH; "they have set up their
detestable things in the house which bears My name, to
defile it. They have built the high places of Tofet in the
Ben-Hinnom Valley, to burn their sons and daughters in
the fire, something I never ordered; in fact, such a thing
never even entered My mind! Therefore, the days are
coming," says YeHoVaH, "when it will no longer be
called either Tofet or the Ben-Hinnom Valley, but the
Valley of Slaughter — they will put the dead in Tofet,
because there will be no space left. The corpses of this
people will become food for the birds in the air and the
wild animals; no one will frighten them away. Then in
the cities of Judah and the streets of Jerusalem I will
silence the sounds of joy and gladness and the voices of
bridegroom and bride; because the land will be reduced
to ruins."*

The people of Judah and Jerusalem failed to heed this warning and just as they were told, The Temple and Judah and Jerusalem were destroyed and the people sent into exile.

Just as those of Judah and Jerusalem should have paid attention to the warning given, we need to heed the warnings of YeHoVaH. We are in the period of the last beast. The beast is taking form and will soon begin to dominate this world as we are told. In Daniel, we are told that this last beast would be different than the previous beasts. It will be more ruthless, cold and destructive than any before it. It will devour the whole earth, trample it down and crush it (Daniel 7:23). The worldwide events taking place today are the continuation of the making of the coming last beast kingdom. This last beast kingdom will come about as the wars, famine and plagues we are experiencing today continue and intensify. The capitalist economic system incorporated into the Greek democratic governing bodies controlled by the elites of the various geographic regions of the world, which even the Chinese elite will eventually be persuaded to join (the Chinese will claim their system has always been "for the people" and thus democratic), will come to completely dominate the world. The economic development made possible by capitalism and the blinders provided by the religious leaders to the people will so obscure everyone's understanding and beliefs that even as the events told to us in Revelation 9 take place, people will not turn to YeHoVaH for help or love. Further disaster will strike the earth and YeHoVaH will begin to bring these events to a close. Revelation 10 The two witnesses will then appear in Jerusalem and begin delivering their message (Revelation 11:3-13). After the two witnesses deliver their message, they are called by God up into heaven. At this point, the last beast shall have come together and begun its reign on earth. The world's religious leaders will assist the beast in making the populous comply (Revelation13). The last beast kingdom lead by the anti-Christ will engage in war with the holy ones and the Lamb (Daniel 7, Revelation 17). After initial success, the last beast kingdom will be defeated.

Revelation 19:1-21 *"After these things, I heard what sounded like the roar of a huge crowd in heaven, shouting,*

"Halleluyah! The victory, the glory, the power of our God! For His judgments are true and just. He has judged the great whore who corrupted the earth with her whoring. He has taken vengeance on her who has the blood of His servants on her hands."

 And a second time they said,

"Halleluyah! Her smoke goes up forever and ever!"

 The twenty-four elders and the four living beings fell down and worshipped God, sitting on the throne, and said,

"Amen! Halleluyah!"

A voice went out from the throne, saying,

"Praise our God, all you His servants, you who fear Him, small and great!"

 Then I heard what sounded like the roar of a huge crowd, like the sound of rushing waters, like loud peals of thunder, saying,

"Halleluyah! YeHoVaH, God of heaven's armies, has begun His reign! "Let us rejoice and be glad! Let us give Him the glory! For the time has come for the wedding of the Lamb, and His Bride has prepared herself —fine linen, bright and clean has been given her to wear."

("Fine linen" means the righteous deeds of God's people.)

The angel said to me, "Write: 'How blessed are those who have been invited to the wedding feast of the Lamb!'" Then he added, "These are God's very words." I fell at his feet to worship him; but he said, "Don't do that! I'm only a fellow-servant with you and your brothers who have the testimony of Yeshua. Worship God! For the testimony of Yeshua is the Spirit of prophecy."

Next I saw heaven opened, and there before me was a white horse. Sitting on it was the one called Faithful and True, and it is in righteousness that He passes judgment and goes to battle. His eyes were like a fiery flame, and on His head were many royal crowns. And He had a name written which no one knew but Himself. He was wearing a robe that had been soaked in blood, and the name by which He is called is, "THE WORD OF GOD." The armies of heaven, clothed in fine linen, white and pure, were following Him on white horses. And out of his mouth comes a sharp sword with which to strike down nations — "He will rule them with a staff of iron." It is He who treads the winepress from which flows the wine of the furious rage of YeHoVaH, GOD of heaven's armies. And on His robe and on His thigh He has a name written:

KING OF KINGS

AND

LORD OF LORDS.

Then I saw an angel standing in the sun, and he cried out in a loud voice to all the birds that fly about in mid-heaven, "Come, gather together for the great feast God is giving, to eat the flesh of kings, the flesh of generals, the flesh of important men, the flesh of horses and their riders and the flesh of all kinds of people, free and slave, small and great!" I saw the beast and the kings of the earth and their armies gathered together to do battle with the rider of the horse and His army. But the beast was taken captive, and with it the false prophet who, in its presence, had done the miracles which he had used to deceive those who had received the mark of the beast and those who had worshipped his image. The beast and the false prophet were both thrown alive into the lake of fire that burns with sulfur. The rest were killed with the sword that goes out of the mouth of the rider on the horse, and all the birds gorged themselves on their flesh."

After the destruction of the manmade system and the defeat of the beast kingdom, the Messiah of YeHoVaH begins His reign on earth for one thousand (1000) years.

Revelation 20:1-15 "Next I saw an angel coming down from heaven, who had the key to the Abyss and a great chain in his hand. He seized the dragon, that ancient serpent, who is the Devil and Satan [the Adversary], and chained him up for a thousand years. He threw him into the Abyss, locked it and sealed it over him; so that he could not deceive the nations any more until the thousand years were over. After that, he has to be set free for a little while. Then I saw thrones, and those seated on them received authority to judge. And I saw the souls of those who had been beheaded for testifying about Yeshua and proclaiming the Word of God, also those who had not worshipped the beast or its image and had not received the mark on their foreheads and on their hands. They came to life and ruled with the Messiah for a thousand years. (The rest of the dead did not come to life until the thousand years were over.) This is the first resurrection. Blessed and holy is anyone who has a part in the first resurrection; over him the second death has no power. On the contrary, they will be cohanim of God and of the Messiah, and they will rule with Him for the thousand years. When the thousand years are over, the Adversary will be set free from his prison and will go out to deceive the nations in the four quarters of the earth, Gog and Magog, to gather them for the battle. Their number is countless as the sand on the seashore; and they came up over the breadth of the Land and surrounded the camp of God's people and the city He loves. But fire came down from heaven and consumed them. The Adversary who had deceived them was hurled into the lake of fire and sulfur, where the beast and the false prophet were; and they will be tormented day and night forever and ever. Next I saw a great white throne and the One sitting on it. Earth and heaven fled from His presence, and no place was found for them. And I saw the dead, both great and small, standing in front of the throne. Books were opened; and another book was opened, the Book of Life; and the dead were judged from what was written in the books, according to what they had done. The sea gave up the dead in it; and Death and Sh'ol gave up the dead in them; and they were judged, each according to what he had done. Then Death and Sh'ol were hurled into the lake of fire. This is the second death — the lake of fire. Anyone whose name was not found written in the Book of Life was hurled into the lake of fire."

A new heaven and new earth are provided.

Revelation 21:1-27 *"Then I saw a new heaven and a new earth, for the old heaven and the old earth had passed away, and the sea was no longer there. Also I saw the holy city, New Jerusalem, coming down out of heaven from God, prepared like a bride beautifully dressed for her husband. I heard a loud voice from the throne say, "See! God's Sh'khinah is with mankind, and He will live with them. They will be His people, and He Himself, God-with-them, will be their God. He will wipe away every tear from their eyes. There will no longer be any death; and there will no longer be any mourning, crying or pain; because the old order has passed away." Then the One sitting on the throne said, "Look! I am making everything new!" Also He said, "Write, 'These words are true and trustworthy!'" And He said to me, "It is done! I am the 'A' and the 'Z,' the Beginning and the End. To anyone who is thirsty I myself will give water free of charge from the Fountain of Life. He who wins the victory will receive these things, and I will be his God, and he will be My son. But as for the cowardly, the untrustworthy, the vile, the murderers, the sexually immoral, those involved with the occult and with drugs, idol-worshippers, and all liars — their destiny is the* *lake burning with fire and sulfur, the second death." One of the seven angels having the seven bowls full of the seven last plagues approached me and said, "Come! I will show you the Bride, the Wife of the Lamb." He carried me off in the Spirit to the top of a great, high mountain and showed me the holy city, Jerusalem, coming down out of heaven from God. It had the Sh'khinah of God, so that its brilliance was like that of a priceless jewel, like a crystal-clear diamond. It had a great, high wall with twelve gates; at the gates were twelve angels; and inscribed on the gates were the names of the twelve tribes of Israel. There were three gates to the east, three gates to the north, three gates to the south and three gates to the west. The wall of the city was built on twelve foundation-stones, and on these were the twelve names of the twelve emissaries of the Lamb. The angel speaking with me had a gold measuring-rod with which to measure the city, its gates and its wall. The city is laid out in a square, its length equal to its width. With his rod he measured the city at 1,500 miles, with length, width and height the same. He measured its wall at 216 feet by human standards of measurement, which the angel was using. The wall was made of diamond and the city of pure gold resembling pure glass. The foundations of the city wall were decorated with all kinds of precious stones — the first foundation stone was diamond, the second sapphire, the third chalcedony, the fourth emerald, the fifth sardonyx, the sixth carnelian, the seventh chrysolite, the eighth beryl, the ninth topaz, the tenth chrysoprase, the eleventh turquoise and the twelfth amethyst. The twelve gates were twelve pearls, with each gate made of a single pearl. The city's main street was pure gold, transparent as glass. I saw no Temple in the city, for YeHoVaH, God of heaven's armies, is its Temple, as is the Lamb. The city has no need for the sun or the moon to shine on it, because God's Sh'khinah gives it light, and its lamp is the Lamb. The nations will walk by its light, and the kings of the earth will bring their splendor into it. Its gates will never close, they stay open all day because night will not exist there, and the honor and splendor of the nations will be brought into it. Nothing impure may enter it, nor anyone who does shameful things or lies; the only ones who may enter are those whose names are written in the Lamb's Book of Life."*

What those that obey Torah and the Commands of YeHoVaH and trust Yeshua as Messiah will receive, everlasting love and care.

Revelation 22:1-21 *"Next the angel showed me the river of the water of life, sparkling like crystal, flowing* *from the throne of God and of the Lamb. Between the main street and the river was the Tree of Life producing twelve kinds of fruit, a different kind every month; and the leaves of the tree were for healing the nations — no longer will there be any curses. The throne of God and of the Lamb will be in the city, and His servants will worship Him; they will see His face, and His name will be on their foreheads. Night will no longer exist, so they will need neither the light of a lamp nor the light of the sun, because YeHoVaH, God, will shine upon them. And they will reign as kings forever and ever. Then he said to me, "These words are true and trustworthy: YeHoVaH, GOD of the spirits of the prophets, sent His angel to show His servants the things that must happen soon."*

"Look! I am coming very soon. Blessed is the person who obeys the words of the prophecy written in this book!" Then I, John, the one hearing and seeing these things, when I heard and saw them, I fell down to worship at the feet of the angel showing them to me. But he said to me, "Don't do that! I am only a fellow-servant with you and your brothers, the prophets and the people who obey the words in this book. Worship God!" Then he said to me, "Don't seal up the words of the prophecy in this book, because the time of their fulfillment is near.

"Whoever keeps acting wickedly, let him go on acting wickedly; whoever is filthy, let him go on being made

filthy. "Also, whoever is righteous, let him go on doing what is righteous;

and whoever is holy, let him go on being made holy."

"Pay attention!" "I am coming soon, and My rewards are with Me to give to each person according to what he has done. 13 I am the 'A' and the 'Z,' the First and the Last, the Beginning and the End." How blessed are those who wash their robes, so that they have the right to eat from the Tree of Life and go through the gates into the city! Outside are the homosexuals, those involved with the occult and with drugs, the sexually immoral, murderers, idol-worshippers, and everyone who loves and practices falsehood. "I, Yeshua, have sent my angel to give you this testimony for the Messianic communities. I am the Root and Offspring of David, the bright Morning Star. The Spirit and the Bride say, 'Come!' Let anyone who hears say, 'Come!' And let anyone who is thirsty come — let anyone who wishes, take the water of life free of charge." I warn everyone hearing the words of the prophecy in this book that if anyone adds to them, God will add to him the plagues written in this book. And if anyone takes anything away from the words in the book of this prophecy, God will take away his share in the Tree of Life and the holy city, as described in this book. "The one who is testifying to these things says, 'Yes, I am coming soon!'"

Amen! Come, Lord Yeshua!

May the grace of the Lord Yeshua be with all!

Chapter XIV

Our Last Chance

God is real. He created ALL things. He shows us this every day. If we are honest with ourselves, this fact is confirmed each day as we simply look around at all the wonders we see in this world. We also know He is real because He has told us of His existence. Through His WORD, YeHoVaH – God our Creator – tells us of His existence and tells us one such way we can know and trust this as true. In Isaiah 46, YeHoVaH declares that He and only He, tells us the end at the beginning. He has done just that.

One of the most compelling declarations He presented in His WORD was that, well before Israel had sinned and the Temple built by Solomon was destroyed and Israel disbursed, YeHoVaH through His prophet Isaiah told all that the Temple of Israel and Israel itself would be rebuilt through a man named Cyrus. This was told in Isaiah 44 and Isaiah 45. This declaration was made approximately one hundred years before Cyrus was born. Cyrus did exactly what YeHoVaH said Cyrus was going to do.[58]

Sadly, even with all that is before us, most still do not believe. Even most of those who profess some type of belief in God, do not take the time to read His WORD and let His Spirit guide them to His truth.

YeHoVaH's love for us is so great however, that He still seeks to know us and for us to know Him. He has a plan for salvation of ALL who will seek Him. It is truly as simple as the first command given to our ancestors Adam and Eve. We must trust and obey YeHoVaH. We must obey His Torah and Commands as set forth in His Holy WORD and trust that Yeshua, His Son, is Messiah and Lord of this earth. We can come to this understanding by trusting His WORD and not the words, dictates and / or traditions of men.

---

[58] See **Why did king Manasseh have Prophet Isaiah killed? - Answers**; https://www.britannica.com/biography/Cyrus-the-Great

The first chapter of the Book of Romans presents facts as relevant today as the day they were first written:

Romans 1:1-32 *"From: Paul, a slave of the Messiah Yeshua, an emissary because I was called and set apart for the Good News of God.*

God promised this Good News in advance through His prophets in His WORD. It concerns His Son —descended from David physically; he was powerfully demonstrated to be Son of God spiritually, set apart by his having been resurrected from the dead; he is Yeshua the Messiah, our Lord. Through him we received grace and were given the work of being an emissary on his behalf promoting trust-grounded obedience among all the Gentiles, including you, who have been called by Yeshua the Messiah.

To: All those in Rome whom God loves, who have been called, who have been set apart for Him:

Grace to you and shalom from God our Father and the Lord Yeshua the Messiah.

First, I thank my God through Yeshua the Messiah for all of you, because the report of your trust is spreading throughout the whole world. For God, whom I serve in my spirit by spreading the Good News about His Son, is my witness that I regularly remember you in my prayers; and I always pray that somehow, now or in the future, I might, by God's will, succeed in coming to visit you. For I long to see you, so that I might share with you some spiritual gift that can make you stronger — or, to put it another way, so that by my being with you, we might, through the faith we share, encourage one another. Brothers, I want you to know that although I have been prevented from visiting you until now, I have often planned to do so, in order that I might have some fruit among you, just as I have among the other Gentiles. I owe a debt to both civilized Greeks and uncivilized people, to both the educated and the ignorant; therefore I am eager to proclaim the Good News also to you who live in Rome.

*For I am not ashamed of the Good News, since it is God's powerful means of bringing salvation to everyone who keeps on trusting, to the Jew especially, but equally to the Gentile. For in it is revealed how God makes people righteous in His sight; and from beginning to end it is through trust — as His WORD puts it, "But the person who is righteous will live his life by trust."[a]**

What is revealed is God's anger from heaven against all the godlessness and wickedness of people who in their wickedness keep suppressing the truth; because what is known about God is plain to them, since God has made it plain to them. For ever since the creation of the universe His invisible qualities — both His eternal power and His divine nature — have been clearly seen, because they can be understood from what He has made. Therefore, they have no excuse; because, although they know who God is, they do not glorify Him as God or thank Him. On the contrary, they have become futile in their thinking; and their undiscerning hearts have become darkened. Claiming to be wise, they have become fools! In fact, they have exchanged the glory of the immortal God for mere images, like a mortal human being, or like birds, animals or reptiles!

This is why God has given them up to the vileness of their hearts' lusts, to the shameful misuse of each other's bodies. They have exchanged the truth of God for falsehood, by worshipping and serving created things, rather than the Creator — praised be He forever. Amen. This is why God has given them up to degrading passions; so that their women exchange natural sexual relations for unnatural; and likewise the men, giving up natural relations with the opposite sex, burn with passion for one another, men committing shameful acts with other men and receiving in their own persons the penalty appropriate to their perversion. In other words, since they have not considered God worth knowing, God has given them up

*to worthless ways of thinking; so that they do improper
things. They are filled with every kind of wickedness,
evil, greed and vice; stuffed with jealousy, murder,
quarrelling, dishonesty and ill-will; they are
gossips, slanderers, haters of God; they are insolent,
arrogant and boastful; they plan evil schemes; they
disobey their parents; they are brainless, faithless,
heartless and ruthless. They know well enough God's
righteous decree that people who do such things deserve
to die; yet not only do they keep doing them, but they
applaud others who do the same.*

Romans 1:17 Habakkuk 2:4

We must remember these things as we continue our
walk here on earth.

The manmade kingdom in which we currently live will
be destroyed soon. For those who still think of its
capitalistic system as "good", remember what Yeshua's
disciples did after Yeshua had risen and ascended back
to heaven-Acts 2:44 and what we are told in Zechariah
14:21. Also think about what we are told in Revelation
of those who even when experiencing the curses will not
turn to YeHoVaH Revelation 9:20.

YeHoVaH has provided the WAY for those who will take it. The WORD of YeHoVaH is truth. These words of this book are presented to you in love and hope that those who may shall come to know and believe.

May we all know the love and salvation of Yeshua – HalleluYah!!!